The Secret Ceili

The Secret Ceili

Kaylee O'Shay, Irish Dancer

Rod Vick

Laikituk Creek Publishing

The Secret Ceili

Kaylee O'Shay, Irish Dancer

Laikituk Creek Publishing
North Prairie, Wisconsin

This is a work of fiction. Names, characters, places, and incidents either are the product of the author's imagination or are used fictitiously. Any resemblance to actual persons, living or dead, events, or locales is entirely coincidental.

All rights reserved.
Copyright © 2008 by Rod Vick
Soft Cover Edition Copyright © 2015 by Rod Vick

Cover design Copyright © 2008 by Rod Vick

No part of this book may be reproduced or transmitted in any form or by any means, electronic or mechanical, including photocopying, recording, or by any information storage and retrieval system, without the written permission of the author, except where permitted by law.

ISBN-13: 978-0-6924537-7-3
ISBN-10: 0-6924537-7-6

For my sister, Sheila…
a beloved aunt,
a tireless worker,
my friend,
and most importantly,
a mother

always with love.

What readers are saying about Rod Vick's books...

'Hello Mr. Vick - I'm happy to say my daughter has finally become addicted to books.'
- Kristin Tousignant, Windsor, Ontario

'Here is a book every aspiring dancer should read.'
- Hornpipe Magazine on Kaylee's Choice

'Motivational...inspiring... Finally, dancers can identify with their own hero.'
- Irish Dance Magazine

'Vick does an amazing job of creating suspense. I found myself rushing through other tasks to get back to my reading.
- Christy Dorrity, Irish Central

'Rod Vick's stories are always honest and heartwarming...writing that gets better every book!'
- Kathleen O'Reilly-Wild, editor of Feis America Magazine

'I loved it. I think it's (Fire & Metal) the best Kaylee book yet. Your book has everything!'
- Brenna Briggs, author of Liffey Rivers books

'I think the concept and the book are brilliant.'
- Jeff Winke, author of The PR Idea Book

'My daughter and babysitter both love all your books - we've both got the whole set. I order them online for the next big gift occasion as soon as they're out!'
- Jill Hynes, Ontario, Canada

One

She could feel the blisters forming as she danced, the familiar burning that signals the outer layer of skin has begun to separate from the sensitive under layers.

Kaylee O'Shay danced on.

She had once formed two identical blisters the size of quarters, wretched things that tore open and throbbed, white-hot coals boring mercilessly into the bottom of each foot. Kaylee sensed that today's blisters would be just as large and painful.

She danced on.

When she had been nine, Kaylee recalled getting a sliver in a finger while playing at the gravel pit on the edge of Rosemary. She had biked home in tears, and her mother had fetched the peroxide and a needle. Kaylee remembered how she had wailed and screamed, and in the end, the sliver had been just a little thing, easily removed.

"You'd have thought that sliver was the size of a railroad tie the way you carried on," her mother had said. How things had changed in the past five years.

Kaylee danced on.

And then the music stopped.

"Very nice," said Miss Helen, large and dressed always in shabby, dark sweats and at least sixty. She inclined her head slightly toward the sixteen exhausted young girls. "This was a good practice! You all worked hard!" Then with a clap of her hands, she walked briskly across the wide, wooden dance floor toward the front exit, where she usually retreated for a cigarette between classes. Kaylee hated the smell, which she endured regularly as she passed through Miss Helen's space when entering or exiting Trean Gaoth Academy of Irish Dance. Even during class, the nauseating tobacco stench stood out if Miss Helen passed within a few feet.

Sometimes Kaylee wondered why Annie Delaney, the owner of the school, kept Miss Helen on as an instructor. Weren't teachers supposed to be positive role models? Weren't they supposed to dress nicely? Weren't they supposed to actually *like* children?

On the other hand, Kaylee knew that Miss Helen at one time had been an outstanding Irish dancer. Second in the world, according to a picture that Kaylee had once seen hanging at Golden Academy of Irish Dance in Milwaukee. And in that ancient picture, Miss Helen had appeared almost pretty.

"Time changes us all," Mrs. O'Shay had once said. Kaylee knew this was true not only for Miss Helen, but for herself.

Caitlin Hubbard slid next to Kaylee and the two began the process of removing their soft-soled Irish dance shoes, more commonly known as ghillies. The smile on Caitlin's face instantly turned to disgust. "Gross!"

Kaylee followed her friend's gaze to her own white socks, which bore grotesque blotches of reddish-brown. She reached to remove her right sock.

"Don't!" said Caitlin, holding up a hand like a traffic cop. "We may be best friends, but that doesn't mean we have to share everything!" Then she peeked over the top of her outstretched fingers as if expecting to see an autopsy in progress. "Doesn't it hurt."

Kaylee shrugged. "Maybe a little." In truth, the two bleeding hot spots throbbed.

Now Miss Helen—who could apparently destroy a cigarette in the time it took most people to drink a glass of water—hovered above them. She cast a glance at Kaylee's bloody socks.

"When did you feel the blisters start?"

Kaylee disliked conversations with Miss Helen, who almost always made her feel inferior, even criminal. "About halfway through practice."

Now Miss Helen locked eyes with Kaylee. "It was foolish of you not to stop and put bandages or a pad on them."

Stopping had never been an option. Kaylee would never show weakness to Miss Helen. *She's just waiting for me to fail*, Kaylee often told herself. *But that's not going to happen.*

Miss Helen pointed to Kaylee's feet. "Let me see."

Caitlin's eyes went wide, and she slid off the dance floor onto the carpeted waiting area, her eyes scanning the room for a diversion of some sort. She focused on a group of eight-year-olds warming up with Tara, the youngest of the dance instructors.

Without hesitating, Kaylee slipped off both socks. On the ball of each foot, a puffy red oval had formed and then ripped, leaving a ragged patch of skin that glistened with a crust of blood and pus, and beneath which could be seen a darker red. A second blister—still intact—blossomed next to the smallest toe on her left foot.

Miss Helen squinted at the mess. "I've seen worse."

This assessment persuaded Caitlin that she might be able to stomach a glance—a faulty assumption, judging from the look on her face, which clearly indicated that Kaylee's foot carnage ranked somewhere between open heart surgery and a tour through a slaughterhouse.

"I will get something to clean you up," said the older woman, and she headed off in the direction of the offices.

Caitlin slid closer again but this time avoided looking directly at Kaylee's feet. "You're insane, you know."

Kaylee chuckled. "Because I've got blisters?"

Caitlin resisted the temptation to look. "Because you work so hard that you don't care that you've got blisters."

"You know what they say," said Kaylee good-naturedly. "It's not enough just to want success. You've got to do more than everyone else is doing."

"Who said that?"

"Miss Helen."

Caitlin's lips twisted into a smirk. "For someone who can't stand Miss Helen, you certainly sound a lot like her."

Kaylee wrinkled her nose. "All dancers work hard if they want to be good."

Now Caitlin's face grew more serious. "Not like you. You dance at home."

Kaylee shrugged. "Everyone dances at home."

"You dance for *hours*. You ripped the carpet out of your bedroom so you'd have a wood floor to dance on.

You stretch more than we do here at Trean Gaoth. You run a mile every day."

"Two miles," Kaylee corrected her. "Sometimes three."

"And," Caitlin concluded triumphantly, "you're taking private lessons for an hour each week with the person you hate most!"

It was true. On Sunday afternoons, Kaylee met Miss Helen at Trean Gaoth Academy for one-on-one instruction, a move that Miss Helen had advised six months ago after Kaylee qualified for the Open Prizewinner level in all of her required dance steps. Kaylee decided to not mention that her father had purchased—at her urging—a secondhand set of barbells, which Kaylee had begun using to strengthen her stomach and upper body muscles.

Kaylee looked away from Caitlin, spied one of the bloody socks on the floor, wadded it up and tried to bounce it like a ball. It did not bounce.

"It's no big deal."

On the other hand, Kaylee's hard work had produced astonishing results. She and Caitlin had moved through the first two levels of competitive dancing—Beginner and Advanced Beginner—at about the same rate over a period of three years. Each dancer competed in four required steps—reel, slip jig, treble jig, and hornpipe—and advanced to higher levels by earning top finishes in competitions that sometimes pitted them against thirty or more other girls. It was in the third level last year that Kaylee had begun to edge ahead of her friend, a painful experience for both of them. When Kaylee began to earn first place medals in Open Prizewinner and Caitlin came home with thirds or fourths, tensions between them had built, and for awhile, Caitlin had ignored her friend.

Events in December of the last year had brought them together again—events that Kaylee hardly care to think about. Yet, the terrible episodes replayed themselves in her mind every day, and these thoughts now drew her hand to a pocket in her dance shorts where her fingers closed on a metal disk the size of a half dollar. In the five months since she had come into possession of the disk, Kaylee had immersed herself in dance as if possessed. Caitlin was not the only one who had noticed.

"If you put in as much time on homework, you'd have straight A's," her mother marveled.

"If you'd have stuck with soccer," said her father, who had coached her in youth leagues, "and worked this hard, you'd be a starting forward on the high school varsity as a freshman."

Her Grandma Birdsall—who lived with Kaylee, her parents and her one-year-younger brother, Will—had a different concern. "I think you're going to wear a hole in your wooden floor and end up in the basement!"

Miss Helen, of course, noticed, too.

"You have come a long way in just a few months," said Miss Helen one Sunday afternoon at their one-on-one lesson. "You have first place finishes in two of your four required dances."

That meant that Kaylee was halfway to qualifying for the second-highest competitive level in Irish dance: Preliminary Champion. However, her teacher's next question surprised Kaylee.

"Are you happy?"

At first, Kaylee thought she had misheard the question. What did Miss Helen care about her happiness?

She had always seemed more apt to predict failure for her pupil.

"I know you have been working very hard," Miss Helen said. "I hear the other dancers talking. And you could not move toward Preliminary Champion so quickly if you did not."

All right, so in addition to being a dance instructor and the Incarnation of Evil on Earth, Miss Helen was also part detective. However, Kaylee could still not see what her extra sit-ups had to do with happiness.

"You have become a very good dancer in the past few months," continued Miss Helen, "but something is missing."

"What?" asked Kaylee.

Miss Helen's face betrayed no emotion except for a softening around the eyes. "Your smile."

Kaylee's hand almost went to the metal disk, which was always in her pocket, but she did not want to reveal this intimate detail of her life to Miss Helen.

"When you started dancing four years ago, you smiled all the time," explain the older woman. "Now—never."

Kaylee shrugged. "My dad says it's hormones."

Kaylee almost thought she detected the trace of a smile around the corners of Miss Helen's mouth, but the old woman quickly suppressed her humanity.

"Perhaps."

Then the Sunday lesson had continued. *Great,* Kaylee had thought. *Now she's even critiquing my facial expressions.*

Now her teacher reappeared from the office area of Trean Gaoth Academy, carrying implements that would bring Kaylee still more pain.

"Hold still while I dab with peroxide."

Kaylee felt as if a bullet were being removed. She gritted her teeth to hide her discomfort from Miss Helen, although a grunt seemed to escape through her nostrils at one point.

Her teacher applied antiseptic and bandages, and after a minute, Kaylee was slipping on her grotesque socks once again.

"Make sure they do not become infected!" warned Miss Helen as she retreated toward the offices, almost running into Annie, who was approaching from the opposite direction.

Kaylee had always liked Annie Delaney, who seemed to have words of encouragement for all of her dancers. The owner of Trean Gaoth Academy, Annie was a tall woman in her thirties, with waves of golden hair tied back in a ponytail. She possessed penetrating green eyes behind smallish, oval eyeglasses. Today she wore navy-blue warm-up pants and a gold and navy-blue Trean Gaoth t-shirt.

"Ouch!" said Annie, noticing Kaylee's bloodied socks. "Did Miss Helen take care of you?"

Kaylee nodded.

"I've got something for both of you girls," said Annie, handing Caitlin and Kaylee separate envelopes with a minor ceremonial flourish. "Try to let me know in the next two weeks if you wish to accept the invitation." Then she moved off with additional envelopes toward a couple of other girls who were lacing on their street shoes.

Kaylee looked at her friend, whose eyes had widened noticeably. "Invitation?"

"I'm not going to wait to see what it's all about," said Caitlin, peeling open the envelope and pulling out the sheet of paper inside. Kaylee scooted next to her and read over her shoulder.

"What is it?"

Caitlin's eyes were already two-thirds of the way down the page. "We've been invited to be on a ceili team!" gasped Caitlin. "For the oireachtas!"

Ceili teams were usually groups of eight dancers of about the same age who would perform a team dance in front of the judges. Although ceili teams competed at the dozens of feiseanna—the name for Irish dance competitions—throughout the year, the largest and most prestigious gathering of ceili teams was the oireachtas, which would bring together dance schools from across the Midwest.

And Kaylee knew that being invited to dance on a ceili team at the oireachtas was another sign of achievement as an Irish dancer.

"It says that this year's Midwest Oireachtas is in Columbus!" continued Caitlin, her eyes moving across the letter rapidly. "This is so cool! We're going to the Midwest championships of Irish dance!" She popped to her feet and began a dance that was half Irish jig and half anarchy. Then she noticed that Kaylee was still sitting on the edge of the dance floor, not smiling.

"Aren't you excited?" asked Caitlin, still hopping like insane popcorn.

"You bet," replied Kaylee, her hand moving to the metal disk in her pocket.

Dad must be right. Hormones.

Two

Kaylee's younger brother brought the ball down the left side of the field, deftly passing to a Bullet teammate cutting across the center as a defender closed in. Will—easily the fastest player on his soccer team—sprinted to the corner, put a sweet move on the defender and popped into the open on the left side of the goal box. The ball arrived half a second later and Will sent a rope into the upper right corner of the net.

The crowd cheered, although no one exceeded Tom O'Shay in volume, Kaylee observed. The look on her father's face could not have been more luminous if Will had just been awarded the Nobel Prize for soccer.

"Your brother is definitely going to be a star when he gets to high school in two years," said Jackie Kizobu, hunched forward in a folding chair next to Kaylee on the spectator side of the soccer pitch. "And did you notice? I think he's sort of starting to *look* like Angelo Zizzo!"

Jackie had two entire walls of her bedroom covered with posters of soccer superstar Angelo Zizzo. The fact that Kaylee's best friend from her soccer playing days thought that Will looked like the Italian heartthrob sent a nasty shiver up Kaylee's spine.

"Will's pretty good," Kaylee had to admit. "But he ought to be. My dad's constantly working on skills with him. Whenever he's not at his job, he and Will head off to one of the fields."

Just a few years ago, Tom O'Shay had devoted that sort of attention to his daughter. Kaylee remembered how he had coached her team, the Green Storm, and how proud of her he had been when she had started to play well.

Then Kaylee had seen *Isle of Green Fire*, a spectacular fusion of music and Celtic dance, and she had been hooked. As she was drawn into the world of competitive Irish dance, she simultaneously drifted away from her father's world, which orbited an increasingly distant sun in the soccer galaxy.

"This one's going to be a champion!" Tom O'Shay had proclaimed to his wife when Kaylee was still a toddler, nudging along a tiny, spongy soccer ball. *Well,* thought Kaylee, *that's one dream that's not going to happen.* She emerged from her reminiscences long enough to see Will steal the ball away from a mid-fielder in a red jersey. *I guess maybe Will can be the champion.*

Kaylee turned her attention to Jackie, whose Asian ancestry and long, dark hair made her pretty in a completely different way than most of Kaylee's other friends. "Sorry that we had to drag you along to this game."

Jackie was spending the weekend at Kaylee's since her parents were out of town. Mrs. O'Shay and Grandma Birdsall were both at the Stitchin' Kitchen—Mrs. O'Shay's combination fabric store and coffee shop—on this Saturday morning, and so Jackie and Kaylee had tagged along with Mr. O'Shay to watch the Bullets play the Paavo Pirates. Then, half an hour after Will's game ended,

Jackie's team was scheduled to play on the field behind them.

"I enjoy watching soccer," said Jackie, brushing aside Kaylee's apology, her eyes following Will as he sprinted down the left side. "And it'll be nice to have you here to watch *me* play."

Jackie still played for the Green Storm, though Tom O'Shay no longer coached the team.

"Today's our last game of the spring season," continued Jackie. "In fact, it's my last game *ever* with the Green Storm! In the fall, I'll be trying out for the high school team!" Kaylee could sense her friend's excitement.

"So," came a girl's voice from behind them, "that means today will be your last soccer game *ever!*"

Jackie and Kaylee twisted in their folding seats. Standing a few feet behind them was Heather Chandler in her Green Storm uniform, a soccer ball tucked between her elbow and hip, her eyes dark and full of the worst sort of fourteen-year-old cruelty. Next to her stood her best friend, Brittany Hall, perpetually blonde and smirking.

Heather continued. "Because you'll be one of the first cuts during tryouts for the high school team. Unless you're trying out for water girl."

Brittany, also wearing the Green Storm uniform, laughed. "At least O'Shrimp had sense enough to get out before she embarrassed herself."

Kaylee wanted desperately to burn Brittany with a scathing retort.

Speaking of embarrassing yourself, I noticed you could have scored an easy goal last game if you hadn't tripped over the ball!

Embarrassing? Like when you had this crush on Michael Black, and then he dumped you?

You want to embarrass yourself? Try this! And then Kaylee would leap up and fire off several bars of rocket-fast Irish dance steps, her feet barely perceptible blurs.

But Kaylee could hurt Brittany with none of those things. Brittany Hall was the best athlete at Kennedy Park Middle School—and would one day probably be the best at Rosemary Senior High. Far from being a klutz, she had scored three goals in the Green Storm's last game.

And Michael Black, the hottest fourteen-year-old in the school, had been following Brittany like a puppy dog for the past four years.

Even Irish dance offered Kaylee no effective weapon. While Kaylee had been dancing for tiny Trean Gaoth Academy for the past four years, Brittany Hall was a superstar with the enormous Golden Academy, which had more than 1,000 dancers and seemed to win the top prizes in almost every competition.

So Kaylee sat there seething, while Brittany and Heather exchanged high fives.

"See you on the field, Kizobu," said Heather, turning with Brittany to go. Then she whirled back, a hand partially covering her mouth. "Oh, sorry! Brittany and I will be on the field. *You'll* be on the bench!"

The two girls broke into laughter once more.

Unexpectedly, Jackie smiled. "There won't be room for anyone other than you two anyway. Your bloated egos will fill the entire playing surface."

Heather stopped smiling. "Oh, you're just so clever, aren't you, Kizobu?"

Jackie continued to smile. "Sadly, I can't return the compliment, since my last name appears to be the only word of three or more syllables in your vocabulary."

Heather offered up an obscene gesture. Then Brittany tapped her on the shoulder, and the two girls turned and jogged away.

Jackie turned to face forward again. "Even though I know they're shallow morons who anger quickly when confronted by actual wit, I really don't get much pleasure out of moments like that. Those two are still going to score ninety-five percent of the goals, win ninety-nine percent of the popularity contests and get one hundred and ten percent of the hot guys."

Kaylee possessed no evidence to the contrary. Brittany had been saying and doing mean things to her since their first day of peewee soccer almost a decade ago. It made no sense, of course, since Brittany was beautiful, had money and athletic talent. In every possible way, she surpassed Kaylee.

"Maybe you two just have a personality conflict," Kaylee's mother had once suggested.

Kaylee preferred Jackie's explanation:

"Some people are just plain evil. And then there are some who are even worse than that. Then at the absolute *bottom* of the cesspool we find Brittany and Heather."

Brittany had broken Kaylee's leg during a soccer game, had hidden Kaylee's Irish dance dress so that she could not perform in the school talent show and had stolen Kaylee's ghillies at a dance competition a year ago.

But there had been a moment last fall, when it had seemed that Kaylee and Brittany might become friends. They had carried on conversations that had not involved insults. Kaylee had attended a party at Brittany's house. True, the party had lacked adult chaperones and Kaylee had narrowly avoided being caught when the police busted the event, but for a fleeting nanosecond-sized moment, Kaylee had been . . . popular. Or at least had been drifting across the wide and lonely sea toward that distant shore where the popular people sunned and splashed.

But last fall had been strange and awful in so many ways. Without consciously willing it, Kaylee's fingers again went to the metal disk in her pocket. The crowd roared, and several stood out of their folding chairs. Tom O'Shay's voice boomed above them all. Will had scored again.

This one's going to be a champion.

Kaylee's fingertips brushed across the raised figures on the disk and pulled it from her pocket. The gold medal had belonged to her Aunt Kat—the prize for winning the conference championship in the 800-meter run when Kat had been a high school senior. Kaylee's throat seemed to tighten as she stared at the award. Her Aunt Kat—so beautiful, so young, so full of energy. She had seemed unstoppable, successful at everything she attempted. Then, last year, she had gotten sick and died.

Kaylee thought about her invitation to be on a ceili team for the Midwest oireachtas.

Maybe there's room for two champions at the O'Shay house.

Soon, Jackie excused herself and headed off to where the rest of her Green Storm teammates were warming up. When Will's game ended, Kaylee's father found her. "I'm going to get Will something to eat at the snack shack. Then we'll come over and watch Jackie's game. You want anything?"

Kaylee shook her head. As Will and her father ambled off, it startled Kaylee to realize that her "little" thirteen-year-old brother was within a few inches of being as tall as Tom O'Shay. She suddenly wished that they could travel backward in time to when her brother was a chubby-faced little cereal addict who played with tiny cars and wooden trains, when she had danced merely because it was beautiful and thrilling and fun, and when her Aunt Kat had been well.

She set her folding chair amongst the seated spectators alongside Jackie's field. The game against the Stampede turned out to be what Kaylee had expected: the Brittany and Heather show. Each scored a goal in the first half, hogging the ball unapologetically. It was as if most of their teammates were invisible. When a teammate messed up, Brittany and Heather berated the girl mercilessly. Somehow the coach, a mousy little balding man with a tiny moustache, seemed to notice none of this. But then, Kaylee remembered how when her own father had coached the Green Storm, he had never seemed to notice Brittany's cruelty, either.

At halftime, the Green Storm led 2-0. While the coach circled his team near the bench and talked strategy, Kaylee noticed that Heather had wandered off to where the water bottles were lined up to get a drink. *Figures. Probably thinks she doesn't need any coaching.*

Kaylee looked to see where Brittany had gone and spotted her a short distance away, waving to a couple of boys in the crowd. The mousy coach looked up, spotted her, and then seemed to pretend that he hadn't, resuming his instruction to the rest of the team. A minute later, the Green Storm broke onto the field and began passing the ball to loosen up. Brittany continued to gab with the boys until the referee's whistle called the starters into position. It was at this point that the two boys turned in Kaylee's direction and she was shocked to discover that one of them was Will.

Was Brittany Hall just flirting with my brother? That's just gross. In fact, that's just one hundred light years beyond gross!

The second half was basically a replay of the first, with Brittany and Heather scoring another goal apiece to put the Green Storm in front 4-0. The coach put Jackie in as a defender with about ten minutes to go. She played well, Kaylee thought, getting right in the face of the Stampede forwards so that they could not get off a clear shot. At least that was how it went until Heather became impatient. Dropping back far out of position, she tried to steal the ball from the Stampede forward, but in the process, collided with Jackie. Both collapsed in a heap, and the open Stampede forward chipped in an easy goal.

"I had her!" cried Jackie angrily.

"You tripped me!" growled Heather. "And you blew our shut-out, you little loser!"

The coach benched Jackie.

After the game, Jackie found Kaylee, but Heather and Brittany trailed just behind.

"You're lucky this is your last game, Fortune Cookie," grunted Heather, "or I'd tell the coach to make you sit the bench the rest of the season!"

Jackie shook her head in disbelief. "Are you really that much of an idiot? Can't you see that they would have never scored that goal if you hadn't been such a ball hog?" Then Jackie rolled her eyes and spoke sweetly, as if to a three-year-old. "What was I thinking? I forgot. You really *are* that much of an idiot!"

Heather's face grew dark and she took a step toward Jackie. Brittany stood just behind, her face impassive except for the eyes, which seemed to radiate a wicked glee. Kaylee felt her hand tighten on Aunt Kat's medal. She stepped beside Jackie. "If you have a problem with my friend, you've got a problem with me."

"Actually," said Heather, "I've always had a problem with both of you. The only question is: Who wants to get hurt first?"

A boy's voice, deep yet uneven, interrupted them. Kaylee recognized it as her brother's.

"Everything okay over here?"

He was taller than Heather. And Brittany. And the anger had drained from Brittany's face, her eyes now riveted to Will O'Shay. Features softened, the beginnings of a smile. *Oh, wow!* thought Kaylee. *She likes him!*

Heather seemed unaffected by her brother's charms. "Just telling Kizobu that we didn't appreciate how she screwed up our shut-out!"

Will nodded, then looked at Jackie, shrugging. "I thought she played great."

Jackie's eyes popped wide.

Heather seemed unfazed. "She tripped me!"

Will shook his head and smiled as if this were the dumbest thing he had ever heard. "And you tripped her. Guess you're even." Then Will turned to Kaylee and held up a hand. "Dad says we're leaving in five." Kaylee nodded as her brother turned and began walking away.

"C'mon," said a much gloomier Brittany, placing a hand on Heather's shoulder. The two headed back across the field.

"Yup," said Jackie, interrupting Kaylee's thoughts, her eyes following the retreating boy, "your brother is definitely looking a lot like Angelo Zizzo!"

The next thing Kaylee saw were stars. She did not lose consciousness, but the shot to the side of the head sent her to the ground.

"Forgot your soccer ball, Kizobu!" jeered Heather from twenty meters away.

"Oops!" added Brittany, and the two laughed as they turned their backs and continued across the pitch.

Jackie knelt to her friend. "Are you okay?"

Kaylee was not okay. She felt a trickle of blood coming from her left nostril, and the area around her left eye throbbed as if she had been punched. As Jackie helped her to her feet, Kaylee noticed that the damage was even worse than she had first thought.

"The medal!"

Jackie seemed confused by this, but Kaylee quickly explained.

"I had my Aunt Kat's medal in my hand! It must have flown out when I got hit!"

The two dropped to their knees. Blood flecks dotted the grass where Kaylee searched.

"I don't see anything!" said Jackie. "Maybe it flew into the tall grass!"

That seemed likely, since the grass had been mowed to a point only a couple of feet behind where they stood. The tall grass quickly gave way to weeds, vines, sumac and, beyond that a short distance, older trees.

They dug through the brush and wild growth. Mr. O'Shay and Will eventually joined them. "What happened to you?" asked her father, but Kaylee somehow found a way to direct his attention to the search. After forty-five minutes, they still had nothing to show for their efforts. By now the tears had dried on her cheeks, and the blood had crusted around her nostril. Her mother would inform her later that a bruise was starting to form just under her left eye.

"I'm sorry, sweetheart," said her father as they stood facing the well-trampled brush. "If it was findable, I'd think we'd have found it by now."

Jackie gave her a hug. "We can search more."

"No." Kaylee shook her head. "It's gone."

Three

"Money," Tom O'Shay had said, rubbing his thumb and forefinger together meaningfully. "That's the only issue."

The previous night at the dinner table, they had been discussing the economics of going to the Midwest Oireachtas. Money was always the issue at the O'Shay household.

"Don't be frustrated, dear," Mrs. O'Shay had said. "We're going to try to make this work."

But the dinner had ended with no firm answer. Kaylee knew that the other seven girls who had been invited to dance on her team had already returned their invitations to Annie. All had answered yes. Kaylee also knew that if she could not return a yes answer in the next week or two, Annie would be forced to replace her on the team.

That's the way my life has been going lately, she thought. She still had a greenish-purplish-yelllowish blotch beneath her eye from where the soccer ball had caught her a week earlier, but the pain had subsided. Or rather, the *physical* pain was gone. The inner pain caused by the loss of her aunt's medal would remain forever. The medal had represented her aunt's great triumph, had reminded Kaylee of how Aunt Kat had once been healthy and unbeatable. Now, like her aunt, gone forever.

Today, Kaylee swept the wooden floor at the old downtown Rosemary building that housed her mother's business, the Stitchin' Kitchen. While mature women sat at sewing machines near the large front windows—occasionally breaking to visit the coffee bar that rose like an alter in the middle of everything—Kaylee swept the aisles between the bolts of fabric. She occasionally emitted little grunts of frustration, glad to have her dark mood hidden by the shelves.

She hated being the girl who could only dance at a couple of feiseanna each year because the entry fees and hotel stays were so expensive.

She cursed the unfairness of having parents who were not lawyers or bankers or doctors like the parents of so many of her friends in Irish dance. Kaylee's father worked as a custodian at Kennedy Park Middle School. Her mother ran the Stitchin' Kitchen, but most months, she was lucky to break even. This past fall, the store had lost more money than usual because Bethany O'Shay had taken so much time off to tend to her sick sister.

She hissed at the weather. Not today's weather, which poured bright sunlight through the store's front windows, but the snow and ice just a few months earlier in January. It had snowed more than usual in late December and early January, leaving deep, white blankets on every roof on Cranberry Street. According to Kaylee's father, their poorly insulated house leaked copious amounts of heat through the roof, which melted the snow, which ran down the roof and then re-froze into solid ice when it reached the drainage gutters at the unheated roof edge. This "ice dam", as her father referred to it, had then pushed up underneath the edges of the shingles, melted again, and sent cascades of water down the inside walls and through the ceiling of the O'Shay living room. The water had run unabated for three days while the O'Shays busied themselves in Chicago, tying up the details of Aunt Kat's estate. The plaster walls, ceiling, furniture, TV—all had been ruined.

Insurance had helped pay for some of the damage, but not all. Getting the house repaired and replacing the furniture had been expensive and had used up much of the money that Aunt Kat had left to her sister.

"What about the money Aunt Kat left to me?" Kaylee had asked. "Why can't we use that to help pay for my trip to oireachtas?"

Bethany O'Shay mother had shaken her head. "Aunt Kat was very clear about how that money was to be used. It's for college, period. If we start borrowing a little here and a little there, who knows where it will end?"

Not even Grandma Birdsall, who lived in the spare room, could help. She had paid for Kaylee's Irish dance lessons and occasionally shored up the expenses that arose at the Stitchin' Kitchen, but even those things were getting harder for her to do. Her heart condition required more and more of the most astonishingly priced medication, and the insurance company seemed inclined to pay a rapidly declining share of that cost.

"Too bad you don't have a large collection of rare Angelo Zizzo posters like I do," her friend Jackie had said as Kaylee pouted about her dismal fiscal situation. "You could sell them online and make a fortune." Jackie considered her own advice for a moment before adding, "Not that any sane individual would consider selling her Angelo Zizzo posters."

Kaylee had grunted. "If I were you, I'd have parents who were so rich I wouldn't have to sell my posters."

Kaylee's daydreams dissolved as Mrs. O'Shay called from the direction of her office near the front of the building. "Kaylee, come up here!"

She leaned the broom against the end of a shelving unit and trudged toward the bright front. Her mother met her near the coffee bar, carrying Kaylee's dance garment bag.

"Let's try this on. It should fit over the shorts and t-shirt you're wearing."

Kaylee rolled her eyes. "I've worn it a thousand times!"

"I know," said Mrs. O'Shay patiently. "But we have to make sure it fits properly if you're going to be on a ceili team."

Now Kaylee sighed in exasperation. "I'm probably not going to be on a team. We have no money, remember?"

Her mother smiled wearily, draping the garment bag over the edge of the coffee bar and unzipping it. "We haven't given up yet." Kaylee's school dress emerged, eliciting *oohs* and *how beautifuls* from several of the ladies sitting at the sewing machines.

All of the school dresses worn for shows and competitions by Trean Gaoth Academy dancers were identical, made of heavy, navy-blue gabardine with gold trim. Intricate Celtic knots decorated the stiff skirt, and a dove rising above a stylized gust of wind decorated the cape. School dresses were—like everything associated with Irish dance—quite expensive, and that was where Kaylee's grandmother had stepped in. A talented seamstress whose room at the O'Shay house was crammed with fabrics, threads and several sewing and embroidery machines, Grandma Birdsall had sewn a school dress for Kaylee, a dress that had turned out perfect. Normally the dresses were custom ordered, but Annie had allowed Kaylee to use hers since it was an exact replica.

The dress was Kaylee's most prized possession.

Mrs. O'Shay unzipped the back of the dress and held it up. "Here you go!"

Again Kaylee rolled her eyes. "I don't see why I have to try it on. It's my own dress! I've been wearing it, like, forever!"

"Exactly!" said her mother. "Grandma Birdsall sewed this dress three years ago. Don't you think you've grown some since then?"

"But," protested Kaylee as she stepped into the skirt, "I just wore it for the school's St. Patrick's Day shows in March!"

Bethany O'Shay shook her head. "You only danced one of the shows in March, and you wore your solo dress for that one."

Solo dresses, unlike the uniform school costumes, were unique statements, each one different—colorful, shiny, full of frills and personality. Dancers had to earn their solo dresses by winning first place at higher levels of competition. Kaylee's dream was to own a shimmering green solo dress, but she had settled for a very nice secondhand blue dress that they had discovered at a feis the previous year.

"Now that I think about it," continued Kaylee's mother, "you haven't worn your school dress in almost a year. You've been wearing your solo dress to feiseanna since the middle of last summer."

"So?" Kaylee argued. "I'm still the smallest in my class at school! It's not like I've grown—"

She stopped as her hands emerged from the sleeves of her school dress. At least three inches of arm showed above her wrists. She noticed now that the skirt hem hung much higher than previously.

"I could try to finish zipping you up," said her mother as she struggled at the back of the dress, "but I'm afraid we would just break the zipper."

"Grandma will have to let it out again," said Kaylee. "She's done that a couple of times before when I've grown."

Mrs. O'Shay shook her head. "There's no more fabric to let out. This dress is at its limit."

Kaylee felt a small pain in her stomach and tears at the corners of her eyes as the truth dawned on her. The beautiful school dress that her grandmother had worked so hard to make, a dress stitched together with equal amounts of thread and love—Kaylee would never wear it again.

"I was afraid of this," said Mrs. O'Shay heavily.

Kaylee struggled to find words. "What do we do? Can Grandma make me a new dress?"

She knew the answer to that question before it was out of her mouth, but she had to ask. She was not ready to surrender. Grandma Birdsall had been working on a new solo dress for Kaylee for months, but had made little progress. Her heart condition had slowed the work to a crawl. Then when Aunt Kat had become ill, Grandma Birdsall had needed to spend the time with her daughter. Even now, Grandma Birdsall had little energy or enthusiasm for anything, and Kaylee knew that her heart medication was only a small part of the reason.

"I'm sorry, sweetheart," was all Mrs. O'Shay could say.

Then that was it. They could probably not afford all of the normal expenses that surrounded oireachtas. Add the price of a new school dress, and the event was way off the charts.

"Excuse me," said one of the older women sitting at a sewing machine. "How much does a dress like that cost?" She pointed to the school dress, which was now spread on the coffee bar once again."

"About the price of a new washing machine," said Mrs. O'Shay. "Or a dryer. Or both."

The older woman, who wore jeans and a plaid shirt and had beautifully-styled short, graying hair, gestured toward Kaylee but spoke to Mrs. O'Shay. "Is your daughter looking for a part-time job?"

"Yes!" cried Kaylee before her mother could respond.

The woman seemed about ready to say something else, but turned back to squint at Kaylee. "My dear, what happened to your eye?"

Kaylee explained that she had been hit by a soccer ball, although she left out the details of the teen drama that had precipitated the event. Then Mrs. O'Shay approached the subject of the part-time job in a bit more subdued manner than her daughter.

"What did you have in mind?"

The woman smiled kindly. "I own a farm outside of Rosemary." She turned to Kaylee and extended a hand. "I'm Virginia Grant. Actually, I'm retired and my son manages the farm now. But I know he hires several people in the spring to help out over the summer months. I could ask him if he has any openings, if you'd like."

"A farm?" Kaylee was not quite sure what to think of this. She had imagined a job in town, the sort of work some of her friends had found: flipping burgers, making pizza, packing groceries. Picking carrots was not exactly how she had imagined spending her summer. On the other hand, watching all of her friends at Trean Gaoth prepare for oireachtas without her was not how she had imagined spending her summer, either.

"What sort of work would Kaylee be doing?" asked Mrs. O'Shay.

"I'm not sure," said Mrs. Grant. "In fact, my son may have already finished hiring. However, I could have him give you a call with the details if he has any openings."

"Please, yes!" said Kaylee, and after a moment, her mother nodded as well.

"Thank you."

Carrots, peas, strawberries . . . Kaylee knew she would pick anything if it meant she could go to oireachtas.

Four

"All right, from the beginning!" Miss Helen clapped her hands together and the eight girls reassembled in their start positions, two girls standing side-by-side at each of the four positions. The music—"Trip to the Cottage"—started and each girl held the nearest hand of her partner. Suddenly, eight feet snapped into a point position and the four pairs raised their clasped hands in unison.

The dance began.

Kaylee and a girl named Olivia had been paired at the first position and faced Caitlin and Gina. Karen and Joleen danced at her left while Pearce and April danced at the right. All four pairs moved gracefully in a counter-clockwise direction around an imaginary center, then switched direction. They changed partners, split into singles, spun each other, all while executing the most intricate footwork. Several minutes later, the music ended, with all four pairs back in their starting positions. They turned to face the front, bowed, and then walked together toward their teacher.

"Not bad for just your second practice," said Miss Helen. "But you must do these steps on your own, too. You must learn them so that you do them without thinking. That is the easy part. Getting up on the toes, staying on beat, working as a unit—that is what is difficult."

The drilling continued for another half hour.

After Miss Helen had disappeared out the front door for her usual between-classes recreation, the eight sat on the edge of the dance floor unlacing their ghillies. Kaylee knew all of the girls well except for Joleen and Pearce. Joleen, Kaylee quickly learned, possessed a naturally outgoing personality and contributed to the conversation at every opportunity. Pearce was her mirror opposite, a mousy little thing with large eyes and straight, dark hair who seemed reluctant to breathe without permission.

"This is hard!" said Joleen after she felt certain that Miss Helen was outside the double glass doors. "It's like she's watching us constantly!"

"Well, this is teams," said Caitlin, shrugging. "It's not like we're dancing for just ourselves anymore. She's got to make sure we're all doing it right."

Olivia nodded. "And that we're all together."

"I think we looked pretty good today," said April.

Kaylee, who had so far been listening without comment, thrust her ghillies into a duffel bag with a loud sigh. "Not good enough! We're not just training for a St. Patrick's Day performance. This is for the oireachtas. This is important. And if we want to make recalls, we've got to work even harder."

Joleen raised an eyebrow at this. "Who made you the boss?"

Caitlin rushed to Kaylee's defense. "She's not trying to be the boss. She's just telling the truth. If we want to make recalls, we're going to have to really commit!" Miss Helen had estimated that there would be more than sixty teams in their age division. In order to recall, the judges needed to rank a ceili team in the top half.

"That's right," said Kaylee. "That means making all the practices, going through the dance at home by yourself, drilling—"

Joleen lowered the water bottle from which she had just taken a swig. "I thought this was supposed to be fun. That's what everybody said when the invitations were given out."

"Going to Columbus is going to be a blast!" said Caitlin.

"And we get to stay in a hotel!" added Olivia. "For three nights!"

Everyone broke into excited chatter over this, except for Pearce, who simply sat there as if the conversation were being conducted by complete strangers on a topic that bore no relevance to her whatsoever.

"But we've got lots of hard work to do before we get there," said Kaylee.

April laughed. "You sound like Miss Helen!"

Why does everyone keep saying that? Kaylee wondered.

"Who sounds like me?"

They turned to see the real Miss Helen had returned and stood on the carpeted area next to the dance floor, her thick arms folded across her chest. A couple of the girls pointed to Kaylee, who felt her ears grow warm.

Caitlin broke the silence. "She was just saying how we have to work hard."

"For oireachtas," added Olivia.

Miss Helen glanced at Kaylee and then returned her gaze to the group. "That does sound like me. Do you know that if you are one of the top teams at the oireachtas, you can qualify for the North American Championships? Even the World Championships?"

Miss Helen paused to allow the gravity of this knowledge to have its proper effect on her audience. Then Gina spoke.

"Do you really think we can be that good?"

"What I think," said Miss Helen, "is that you should give yourself a chance to be as good as you can be. If you do not work hard, you are cheating yourself out of that chance."

Kaylee tried to stifle a little self-satisfied smirk inspired by the brooding expression that had appeared on Joleen's face. However, it evaporated a moment later when Miss Helen asked her a question.

"By the way, Kaylee, may I see you in my office?"

She slipped on her running shoes, laced them quickly and followed Miss Helen to the office area across the carpet. The building that housed Trean Gaoth Academy had once been a bowling alley. A broad wooden dance floor had been built over where the eight alleys had formerly been. The carpeted bar and games room area at the front had been partitioned into several small rooms, one of which served as an office for Annie Delaney. There was also a shared room for Miss Helen and Tara, the other two instructors, as well as a storage room. The rest of the carpeted area had been left open as a waiting area and lobby.

The room Kaylee entered featured a single table that served as a desk for both Miss Helen and Tara. A file cabinet sat behind it, as well as a wide bookshelf onto which papers and folders had been stacked. Several dance posters, including one for *Isle of Green Fire*, hung from the walls. Tara was out on the dance floor prepping her next class, and so Kaylee and Miss Helen were alone.

"I noticed," said Miss Helen, "that all of the other girls had returned the forms that they received with their invitations. But yours is still missing. I imagine that I will be receiving it soon?"

Kaylee looked at the floor. "I'll try to have it by next week."

She did not have to see Miss Helen's face; the tone of her voice communicated her confusion. "Are you a bit forgetful? Or are your parents not sure they wish to sign the form?"

Kaylee hated this feeling. Miss Helen thought she was going to let down the team. Although the old woman pushed Kaylee hard in training and even seemed to admit that she was making significant progress as an Irish dancer, there always seemed to be a part of her waiting in the background, a part that knew Kaylee would eventually fail. And Kaylee hated giving Miss Helen any evidence that might justify her suspicions.

Or more precisely, any *additional* evidence.

In her very first year of Irish dance, Kaylee had skipped the big St. Patrick's Day show in which almost all the Trean Gaoth dancers performed. Instead, Kaylee had decided to play in a soccer tournament.

Miss Helen hated soccer. Everyone at Trean Gaoth Academy knew why. Nineteen years ago, Miss Helen had been a dance instructor at Golden Academy where she had trained a talented young girl named Lizzie Martin. Miss Helen had poured tremendous energies into making Lizzie a champion, and it was widely believed that she would place among the elite at the world championships. Then, Lizzie had suddenly quit Irish dance in favor of soccer.

And so Miss Helen was not particularly happy when, in Kaylee's second year, she had missed her first feis because she had broken her leg in a soccer game—or it might have been more accurate to say that *Brittany* had broken her leg. This was, in fact, after Miss Helen had advised her against playing.

And in her third year, Kaylee had danced poorly in almost every competition. While soccer had played no role in her dismal performances, Kaylee knew that her sorry results had surely reinforced the impression with Miss Helen that Kaylee O'Shay would ultimately find a way to disappoint.

But she would not disappoint Miss Helen. She would not let this cruel, unfeeling old woman win.

"I didn't forget it. I'll have it by next week."

She could have told Miss Helen that her family was not certain they could afford all of the expenses that would come with a trip to the oireachtas. She could have mentioned that she was hoping to get a job at Grant Farms. In her heart, though, Kaylee knew that this was unlikely. It had been more than a week since she had spoken with Mrs. Grant at the Stitchin' Kitchen, and no one from Grant Farms had called. If her son had been hiring additional summer help, he would not wait until the second week in June.

Kaylee might have told these things to Annie or even to Tara. But she would not tell them to Miss Helen.

"All right," nodded the old woman. "But Kaylee, I hope you understand our situation. We need the members of our ceili teams to make a strong commitment. If you cannot do this soon, we may have to find someone else to take your spot."

Kaylee felt a flash of panic in her chest, but she betrayed no emotion to Miss Helen. She fought to hold back tears as she grabbed her duffle bag and headed to the parking lot where her mother sat reading a book in the car. Unlike many parents who sat in chairs in the Trean Gaoth lobby during practices, chatting or reading, Kaylee's mother seemed uninterested in what transpired within the building. Today, however, Kaylee's father had dropped her off at practice, and Mrs. O'Shay had arrived sometime later to provide the ride home.

"How was practice, sweetheart?" asked Mrs. O'Shay.

Kaylee's offered a dispirited "Fine."

Mrs. O'Shay started the car as Kaylee fastened her seatbelt. She eyed Kaylee warily while edging the car onto the highway. "You don't sound fine. You sound like you just lost your best friend."

In a way, Kaylee felt like she had. Caitlin would be going to oireachtas. Kaylee would not. That meant they would soon start separate practices. And since Caitlin attended school in Paavo while Kaylee was enrolled in Rosemary, they would hardly ever be together.

And Kaylee was always conscious of having lost Aunt Kat, her other best friend. Her hand automatically moved to her pocket before she remembered that the medal was gone.

"I'm just tired," Kaylee finally replied. She felt like adding, "and poor," but she knew that this would only make her mother feel more guilty. "I think when I get home I'll just crawl right into bed. And maybe watch *Isle of Green Fire*."

"You need to do a load of your laundry first," said her mother. "I think I've seen you wear that t-shirt at least two other days this week."

Kaylee nodded glumly.

"Oh, and you got a phone call from some boy," added Mrs. O'Shay.

Kaylee perked up a bit at this news. "A boy?" She wondered whether it might be Riley, her cute friend from Golden Academy. "Who was it?"

Mrs. O'Shay shrugged. "Your brother took the call. He said the name was Bob and you're supposed to call back."

Kaylee knew two Bobs from school. One was a wrestler who had been in most of her eighth grade classes at Kennedy Park Middle School. The other she had met during rehearsals for the talent show when she was in seventh grade. He was a nice guy with sandy hair who had sung a song from some popular musical, and she had talked with him occasionally about Irish dance. Maybe Bob Not The Wrestler had called to talk. Or perhaps to ask her to a movie.

Sudden panic.

"When did Bob call?"

Mrs. O'Shay thought for a moment. "Middle of the afternoon, I think. I suppose Will wrote down the number and then went back to his video games and forgot to say anything. Not that either of us should be surprised at that." She offered a quick smile.

The middle of the afternoon? What if Bob had wanted to ask her to a movie for tonight? If Kaylee had returned the call at three or four o'clock, they might have arranged their plans for after her dance practice. Now, however, it was surely too late, all because her stupid brother was addicted to stupid games that were a complete waste of time and which now may have actually ruined her life.

As soon as the car stopped in the O'Shay driveway, Kaylee burst out and ran to the telephone in the kitchen where she found the scrap of paper with the word "Bob" and the number. Her brother stood near the sink chewing, a hand buried inside a box of breakfast cereal.

"Thanks a lot!" Kaylee snarled, holding aloft the scrap. "Why didn't you tell me right away?" She felt like throwing the telephone at his head. The thought that it might break and prevent her from returning the call helped her avoid committing a felony.

Will shrugged and spoke through the cereal remnants. "I was busy. Almost at level seventy-eight."

Kaylee rolled her eyes.

"Besides," Will continued. "He said it wasn't an emergency."

Kaylee relaxed a bit. All right, so it probably wasn't an invitation to do anything that evening. Will brushed past her carrying the cereal box and headed up the stairs to his room where the defense of the universe could continue. Kaylee dialed the number anxiously and, after several rings, a man answered.

"I'd like to speak to Bob."

"This is Bob," said the man.

I must have gotten his father, Kaylee thought. "I'd like to talk to the younger Bob, please," she said sweetly.

"Unless you have the wrong number, I'm the youngest Bob you're going to find around here."

Kaylee did not know what to say for a few moments.

"Hello?" Bob's husky voice roused her. She heard what seemed to be the rustling of paper in the background. "Is this Kaylee?"

Kaylee nodded and then realized that he could not see this over the phone. "I was supposed to call Bob," she finally stammered.

"This is Bob Grant," said the man. "I think my mother ran into you in some store downtown."

"The Stitchin' Kitchen," Kaylee said.

"She said you need a job. Can you start on Tuesday?"

Now Kaylee felt even more excited than if it had been Bob Not The Wrestler asking her to go to a movie. "Yes!"

"It'll be hard work."

Kaylee did not care. A job meant money. Money meant she could go to oireachtas.

And it meant that Miss Helen was not going to win.

Five

The cool morning air made Kaylee glad she had pulled on an old sweatshirt before hopping onto her bike. Although the sun had easily cleared the horizon, its rays still angled too severely to offer much warmth.

I should be sleeping until noon.

Instead, she was two miles outside of Rosemary with another to go before she would reach Grant Farms.

I'll be able to go to oireachtas, she told herself. She danced for hours each day, did hundreds of stomach crunches each week and had run hundreds of miles in the past six months. This was simply one more boulder to scale on the way to the top of the mountain.

The top of the mountain . . .

Her Aunt Kat had applied the metaphor to virtually every challenge she had faced in life. Kaylee thought again of the missing medal and then quickly put it out of her mind as she felt the tightening in her chest. She increased her speed, crested a small hill and then coasted down a long slope to the tree-lined driveway marking the entrance to the farm. She turned, passed a large pile of stones out of which stood two wooden posts supporting the GRANT FARMS sign. Her tires slipped as they encountered gravel, and she rose off the seat to apply more pressure to the pedals. After another half mile, Kaylee reached a turnaround flanked by a large farmhouse on one side and a great red barn on the other.

Kaylee lowered her bike into the grass beside the turnaround. She removed her helmet and ran her hands through her wavy, copperish hair, which her mother had tied up with a bandanna. Rubbing an unidentifiable bit of something out of the corner of an eye, she took a closer look at her surroundings. The house stood at the right-hand side of the turnaround, yellow with white shutters and green window boxes from which grew multi-colored pansies. A chest-high cedar rail fence stood in front of the house. A stone walkway passed through an opening in the fence on the way to the front door, flanked by half a dozen iron shepherds' crooks driven into the ground as holders for hanging plants. The great barn dominated the other side of the turnaround, red and wooden and needing new paint. An earthy vinegar smell hung in the air.

What did I get myself into? Kaylee asked herself as she stood on the tough, dry grass at the edge of the turnaround. The sun cast long shadows and Kaylee shivered. Although the ride from town had seemed to wake her up, her eyes suddenly felt heavy again. A cow lowed somewhere in the distance, and Kaylee pictured herself sitting on a stool with a milk pail next to her. When she returned her gaze to the farmhouse, she found Mrs. Grant striding toward her.

"Good to see you, Kaylee! Glad it all worked out with Bob."

At the time Bob Grant had called, all Kaylee had been able to think about was the money she would make to finance her oireachtas venture. He had asked her to arrive by seven in the morning. At the time, midnight would not have sounded too early. Now, however, faced with the reality of her fatigue and the long day before her, noon sounded about right.

Mrs. Grant steered her toward the barn, chatting about the farm as she went. "We don't plant as much as when my father owned the farm. Bob leases a couple of hundred acres to other farmers. We still do some corn and soybeans and potatoes. Lots of hay and wheat."

Kaylee smiled and nodded, not knowing quite what to say. Was she going to have to pick corn? Or did they have a machine for that? They didn't expect her to drive a tractor, did they? She wouldn't even be able to take driver's education in school for another year and a half. But maybe you didn't need a driver's license to operate a tractor.

"I brought work gloves," said Kaylee suddenly, pulling a pair with a flower-print design out of her back pocket.

Mrs. Grant smiled. "Those may come in handy."

As they neared the barn, a small side door opened and a dark-haired man in a tan shirt, jeans and work boots emerged. He wore an uneven stubble of beard, looked to be about ten years older and much taller than her own father. Then again, almost everyone was much taller than the O'Shays. According to her father, Great-Great-Grandpa O'Shay had gambled away his fortune, and when he built the family's ancestral home in Ireland, he could only afford enough wood to make the ceiling five feet ten inches tall. As a result, the O'Shay family had been cursed with shortness.

"Oh, good," said Mrs. Grant. "I was just coming to look for you! Bob, this is Kaylee!"

Kaylee offered her hand, which seemed tiny when Bob shook it with his enormous one.

"So you're my new farmhand!" said Bob in a booming voice. Creases lined his red face and his blue eyes seemed to radiate a skepticism that bore right through Kaylee. She had seen this look before in Miss Helen, and it immediately placed her on the defensive.

"Yes sir," said Kaylee, noticing that she no longer felt tired. Adrenaline coursed through her, generating impatience. "Will I be picking vegetables?"

Bob's eyes narrowed as if he were assessing the meager qualifications of his new charge. "June is a little early for most of our crops. And we have machines that do a lot of the actual grunt work."

Mrs. Grant took this as a good time to leave. "See you at lunch," she called to her son.

"I thought," Bob continued warily, "that you might be a good replacement for Amber."

"Who's she?" asked Kaylee.

Bob puffed out his chest and grunted. "She's my little girl. Though she's not so little anymore, I guess. Just graduated from Rosemary High. She's going to college in Minneapolis in the fall and had an opportunity to get an apartment and a part-time job there at the start of the summer. She took the truck so she could move some stuff up there this past weekend. Supposed to be back tonight, so she can show you how to do her chores when you come tomorrow."

Kaylee looked around. "Isn't there anything for me to do now?"

Bob squinted at her as if examining an insect dangling from tweezers. "There's always something to do on a farm! Plenty for my regular crew. You're here to take care of the little things so they don't have to waste their time on 'em."

He turned abruptly and made a motion that seemed to indicate that Kaylee should follow. The ground gradually sloped toward a small fenced-in yard in back of the barn. Inside the wooden fence, the ground seemed to have been churned up. A couple of windows and two doors—one which was double-wide—were set into the thick stone walls of the barn's foundation and faced this enclosure. The earthy vinegar smell seemed stronger here.

Bob opened a latched gate and led Kaylee to a shovel that leaned against the fence. Nearby stood a four-wheeled metal cart. He grabbed the shovel as if it were a soda straw. "Ever use one of these before?"

Kaylee had shoveled snow. She had also used a much smaller version in the sandbox when she was younger, and so she nodded.

Bob gave her an I'll-bet look and then indicated a dark heap on the ground. "Gotta keep the yard clean." He scooped the pile onto the shovel, took a step toward the cart and deposited the load. Then he made a sweeping gestured around the fenced-in area. "Just keep working your way around, getting it all. I'll check back in an hour to see how you're doing."

Then he retreated through the gate and Kaylee turned to face the job. *I'm shoveling cow plop! To get to oireachtas, I've got to shovel cow plop!*

As she scanned the fenced-in area, she realized the enormity of her task. There seemed to be hundreds of piles. Maybe thousands.

How many cows does this guy have?

Kaylee walked to the nearest mound, jabbed the shovel underneath, got only part of it, heaved it awkwardly into the cart. Bob had made it look so easy. She scooped the rest of the pile. Then she moved on to the next. As she worked the shovel underneath, a horrifying thought occurred to her: What if the cows produced this quantity of waste every day?

Oireachtas! Think of oireachtas!

When Bob returned an hour later, Kaylee had not finished a quarter of the job, and so he ambled off for another hour. By this time, Kaylee had cleared less than half of the yard and felt exhausted.

"Why don't you get a drink at the house?" said Bob, glancing around the enclosure as he spoke.

Kaylee nodded and trudged up the incline. *He probably could have finished in twenty minutes. He's probably thinking how slow I am.*

Mrs. Grant made lemonade and Kaylee drank two big glasses. She also gave Kaylee an oatmeal cookie and asked how the morning was going.

"Real good," Kaylee lied. "Working on a farm is a real experience."

By the time Kaylee slogged back to Bob, the sugar in the lemonade had done its job, and she felt a little better. "I think it's time to take break from shoveling for awhile." He produced a hammer and a carton of galvanized nails. Then he pointed to a small pile of long boards near the latched gate. "How do you feel about doing some fence repair?"

Kaylee felt like it had to be better than what she had been doing for the past two hours.

Bob picked up a long board in one hand and carried it to one of three spots on the fence where a broken board had been removed. He demonstrated how to start a nail, hold the board in place, and then how to finish driving it home. The nail disappeared into the wood in two of Bob's mighty swings. Then he returned to his own work, leaving Kaylee to finish nailing the board he had started.

Kaylee picked up the hammer. *This looks a lot easier than shoveling.*

Tom O'Shay found his daughter asleep on the living room couch when he arrived home from work that evening. Her aromatic, gunk-encrusted jogging shoes had been abandoned near the door leading out to the garage. Her formerly white but now mostly dirty brown socks lay abandoned halfway across the kitchen floor. The sweatshirt made it to the carpet in front of the couch. With her disheveled hair and the dirty streaks on her arms and face, she might have just returned from two weeks in the wilderness.

"Poor dear," said Grandma Birdsall to her son-in-law. "She's been out like a light since she got home a little before one."

He managed to wake her after a few attempts and then fetched a tall glass of orange juice, which Kaylee downed as if it had been served in a thimble.

"I was awful," said Kaylee as her father settled next to her on the sofa. "Everything I did took ten times longer than if they'd done it themselves."

Will came down from his room where he had no doubt been vanquishing aliens from cyberspace. He grabbed an open box of cereal off the kitchen counter, tucked it under his arm and passed near the couch on his way back to the stairs. "You smell funny," he said, pausing just a moment to scrunch his nose at his sister. Then he disappeared back to the battlefield.

"It's probably going to take you some time to adjust to the hard work of farm life," said Tom O'Shay, returning his attention to his daughter.

"Dad, it took me an hour to nail one board!" exclaimed Kaylee. "Five nails!" While the nail had cooperated for Bob as if the wood had been made of pudding, Kaylee found that she hardly noticed a difference after each of her taps with the hammer. "It took me forever, and I think I bent ten nails for every nail that went in straight!"

"Why don't you take a shower," her father said kindly. "You'll feel better about the world after you're cleaned up."

Kaylee acted as if she had not heard him. "Then we went to the upper part of the barn and there was a rusty old pickup truck with a dozen hay bales in the back and I was supposed to pile them with the rest of the bales in the barn. They were heavy!"

Her father listened intently. "Did you have to do it all by yourself?"

Kaylee nodded. "Bob went away and I tried to lift one and I couldn't!"

"I see," said Tom O'Shay slowly.

"But," continued Kaylee, "I could push them. I got up in the truck and put my back against the side and pushed a bale with my legs. I've got strong legs. I pushed it to the back of the truck and it fell off. Then I pushed it over to the big pile and tipped it up on its side. After that, I was able to grab the end on the floor and tilt it up on top of the pile. It took me the whole last hour I was there this morning, but I unloaded all twelve bales."

Mr. O'Shay put an arm around his daughter and squeezed her shoulders. He hoped she had not forgotten about his shower suggestion. "Good for you!"

His daughter's face darkened again almost immediately. "But Bob or anyone else who works there could have unloaded those bales in five minutes! I'm worthless! I wouldn't be surprised if Bob calls you tonight and tells you not to have me come back." The aching and tired part of her was even hoping that this might happen.

Tom O'Shay leaned forward, resting his forearms on his thighs. "Don't be so tough on yourself. Naturally you're going to be slower than big old farm workers who've been doing hard work for years. But it's possible that how fast you work isn't a big deal. Every job you finish is a job that Bob and the others don't have to do. They can devote their attention to other, bigger responsibilities around the farm."

Kaylee sighed. "Maybe."

"Now," said her father, rising from the couch, "I'm going to see whether your grandmother needs any help with supper, since your mother won't be home from the Stitchin' Kitchen until late."

"Great," said Kaylee, who now realized she had not eaten lunch. "I'm starving!"

"But before you do anything else," said Tom O'Shay with a look of urgency in his eyes, "please, take a shower!"

Six

Although Kaylee declared that she was completely exhausted, she did find sufficient energy to have three helpings of everything at supper, including some vegetables that she normally would not eat even when threatened. Even Will, whose voracity usually included demolishing at least one box of cereal per day, seemed impressed.

And she somehow dug deep into her reserves and unleashed a second wind that allowed her to endure an hour-long telephone conversation with Jackie after supper.

"It's the worst possible job ever," Kaylee explained, recounting every horrible detail to her friend. "And my boss is a creepy guy who never smiles and looks at me like I can't do anything right. Which is technically true, I guess, but he's still mean and creepy."

"Your boss sounds like that Neanderthal dance teacher of yours," said Jackie.

"Miss Helen?" Kaylee laughed, remembering her own thoughts during her first moments beneath Bob's intimidating gaze.

"Yeah," said Jackie. "Maybe you should try to get them together!"

She tried to imagine Miss Helen in farm clothes shoveling cow manure. Surprisingly, the image worked.

"Maybe the first day was a test," said Jackie suddenly. "You know. Let's hit her with everything we've got and see if she shows up tomorrow. Then they'll be real nice and give you all sorts of easy jobs like feeding the chickens and baking apple pies."

Kaylee chuckled. "I didn't see any chickens."

"On the other hand," continued Jackie, "what if *today* was the easy jobs and tomorrow they're even worse?"

Kaylee shuddered. "How could they be worse?"

Jackie remained silent for a moment. "Maybe tomorrow they give you a shovel and take you to the *elephant* barn!"

Both girls laughed.

She could not believe the difficulty involved in getting out of bed the following morning. Kaylee hardly tasted her oatmeal and then stood looking at the red bicycle lying in her front yard for several minutes. A part of her wanted to ask her father for a ride to the farm. He would be leaving for work at almost the same time. And he could pick her up during his lunch hour.

She willed the idea out of her mind.

If she wanted to be a champion, she could not take the easy way every time life got tough. Keep climbing that mountain, that's what Aunt Kat would have said.

And so she hopped onto her bicycle and headed down Cranberry Street. Today was cooler than the previous day and heavy-looking gray clouds hung low in the sky. *I'll probably get rained on coming home.* This did not bother Kaylee. Yesterday the bike ride had seemed long, difficult, boring. Today she almost enjoyed it, imagining that these twenty minutes of quiet coolness might be the most pleasant part of her day.

The most pleasant part of her whole summer.

Usually she biked to Jackie's house during the summer. Or Jackie biked to the O'Shay residence. She could sleep late if she wanted. Sometimes she spent the day in downtown Rosemary at her mother's store or walked to the ice cream shop. She practiced dance in her room and watched her favorite Irish dance musical, *Isle of Green Fire*.

This summer would be different. Every day she would be torn from sleep earlier than any of her friends, would bicycle away from the people and places she really enjoyed, and would spend half the day up to her ankles in animal excrement or struggling with monstrous bales or bags of feed or some other grim task that would leave her drained and unable to enjoy the rest of the day.

Oireachtas, she thought, which usually brought an image of herself dancing on a wide stage with her seven ceili teammates in their beautiful school dresses. Today, however, she could only conjure the word.

As she turned onto the gravel drive at Grant Farms, she realized that this was Wednesday, which meant dance practice tomorrow. *I'll hardly be able to move! Miss Helen will probably yell at me the whole practice.* If she appeared too inept, she wondered if Annie would go so far as to drop her from the ceili team.

Kaylee rested her bike against the fence at the turnaround, and she turned toward the house to find a young woman approaching.

"You must be Kaylee. I'm Amber."

Amber Grant was tall like her father, and thick-bodied as well, but not fat. She had straight black hair that hung just past her shoulders and handsome facial features that reminded Kaylee of Amber's grandmother.

Amber looked Kaylee over. "My father says you're not much at mending fences." There was no malice in it, only a smile, yet Kaylee looked at her feet. "But he says you can handle a shovel well enough and he was impressed that you were able to move those bales by yourself. So he thinks you'll do."

Kaylee looked up. *You'll do?* That meant they were not going to fire her. Even though it meant she was sentenced to a summer of hard labor, she felt good about the seeming compliment.

"C'mon," said Amber, turning toward the barn. "We'll get you started."

Kaylee caught up and struggled to keep apace with Amber's long strides.

"Am I going to shovel cow manure in back of the barn again today?" It had been bothering her all night. She imagined that the cows might have restocked the enclosure overnight so that it would appear that she had not shoveled at all.

Amber half turned again, wrinkling her face as if this were an odd question. "We only have two cows, and they don't use that corral."

"Corral?" asked Kaylee. "That's for horses, isn't it?"

"Duh!" said Amber playfully. "Girl, I can tell you're a rookie when you can't tell horse from cow manure!"

Kaylee's pulse quickened. "You have a horse?"

Amber led her down the incline and unlatched the gate to the corral that Kaylee had shoveled the previous morning. "Five horses," said Amber, closing the gate and striding toward the narrower of the two doors set into the mortared stone foundation of the barn. Inside the air was humid with wood and straw and a sweet scent that tickled Kaylee's nose. The floor was uneven concrete, the walls mortared stone like outside with five wooden stalls set at the back. Low rafters held wide planks leaking straw and cobwebs and paint chips.

Kaylee heard the shuffle of hooves and a soft whinny. "Dad said they were out in the west pasture yesterday when you were here. Otherwise you probably would have heard them." She winked at Kaylee. "They do sound a bit different than cows."

Kaylee felt herself blush, but then she craned her neck to try and look past Amber to the large, shifting bodies beyond. Amber noticed this and motioned her forward. "Might as well start getting you acquainted." She led Kaylee to the first of the stalls. "This is Seeley. She's nine, a good girl, very gentle. Aren't you, Seeley?" She was beautiful, thought Kaylee, mostly ivory in color with blotches of black, brown and tan mixed in. She stroked Seeley's long muzzle and patted her side before moving to the next stall, which held a horse with a light brown coat and a sandy-blonde mane.

"Here we have Whiskey. Whiskey needs a firm hand, don't you, boy?" As if the horse understood, it stamped a front hoof on the floor and grunted loudly.

"This one," continued Amber, stepping to stall number three, "is Star. She runs, the barn, don't you, girl? All the other horses seem to take their cues from her, almost like she's the mother of the house."

Star was gray with dapples of darker or lighter pigment about the legs and the face.

"Now here we have Thunder," said Amber, moving to the fourth box. "The name is misleading." She said this as she stroked the animal's face and fed her something from a pocket. "He's almost jet black, but you won't find a more agreeable horse. He's actually our oldest. Has some arthritis and doesn't move around as well anymore."

After a moment, Amber moved to the final stall. "This one's our troublemaker," she said, shaking her head in amusement. "One minute he'll be nice as can be, and the next he'll be biting you in the pants or crying like you dropped a mouse into his feedbag."

The horse shifted anxiously in his stall, brown but darker than Whiskey with a shining, black mane.

"What's his name?" asked Kaylee.

"Trooper," said Amber, offering the horse a carrot. Trooper turned his head as if refusing to perform for this unfamiliar visitor. Amber turned toward Kaylee. "See what I mean? Now if I stop paying attention to him, he'll probably try to—"

With a sudden movement, Trooper turned his head and snatched the carrot out of Amber's outstretched hand. Amber laughed.

"I was going to say that he'll probably try to steal it from me. And there you go!" She rubbed Trooper's nose playfully. Then she looked toward Kaylee. "You'll never get to know them if you stand over there all by yourself!"

Kaylee slid a foot forward tentatively and then walked toward Amber and Trooper. She placed the flat of her palm on Trooper's muzzle and stroked it. "I've never ridden a horse."

Amber laughed. "Before you learn to ride, you've got to learn a few other things." She took a step toward the wall and grabbed a shovel. "Welcome to the exciting world of horse care."

At dinner that night, Kaylee hardly stopped talking to chew.

"I shoveled manure," she announced as the meatloaf made its way around the table. Then she noticed her family's concerned looks. "Don't worry. I showered when I got home. There are five horses." She recited their names. "I fed them, too. And brushed them. And I'm going to learn to pick stuff out of their hooves."

Will looked at his sister as though she might have been kicked in the head by a horse.

"That sounds very nice, dear," said her mother, who really did not think that shoveling manure and picking minutia out of the hooves of large animals fell into the "nice" category, but who was pleased that these things apparently made her daughter happy.

"Shoveling is hard work,' said Tom O'Shay. "You're probably worn out."

Kaylee shook her head. "Oh, no. I feel great!"

And she did feel great. Right up until five minutes after supper when she fell into a dead sleep across her bed with her clothes still on.

Seven

The sound of a morning bird occasionally punctuated the steady beat of her running shoes on the country road. Otherwise, the world unfolded silently around Kaylee O'Shay. Few cars passed at this hour. Dew covered the grass and the sun warmed her legs and forearms when it appeared between the scattered oaks, maples and dogwoods at roadside.

"I'm too tired to run when I get home after working," said Kaylee to her parents. And now she had dance three nights a week as the school prepared for summer shows and oireachtas, which also made it difficult to run in the evening.

"Why do you have to run?" her mother had asked. "You get a good workout on the farm, don't you?"

It was true that the farm was hard work. "But it's not the same. I need to keep my endurance."

That was partly true. Kaylee felt that her running program gave her an advantage that other Irish dancers did not have. But the running also kept her connected to her Aunt Kat, who had run with Kaylee even while she was sick.

So Kaylee ran to the farm every morning—three miles. Mrs. Grant had found her a pair of Amber's old work boots to wear, so Kaylee could spare her running shoes the indignities of the barn or corral. And Kaylee wore a lightweight cloth backpack in which she carried a fresh t-shirt she could change into at the farm, though it would not remain fresh for long. At noon, Mrs. Grant would give Kaylee a ride home.

She passed the one-mile mark, a mailbox in front of a long, dirt drive that disappeared behind a grove of trees at the far end of a cornfield.

"You're certainly a hard worker," Mrs. Grant had said. Even Bob Grant seemed to have been forced to re-evaluate his newest farmhand.

"I think you're going a little overboard," her father had said. She had not expected this response. Usually, Tom O'Shay was the first to trumpet the virtues of hard work and their relationship to athletic success. However, he seemed to think three weeknights of dancing classes, private lessons with Miss Helen on Sunday afternoons, running three miles to work every day, plus the dancing and stretching that Kaylee did at home were too much. "There's no other fourteen-year-old I know of who works this hard."

That, Kaylee thought, was exactly the point.

As her Aunt Kat had often observed, a person could not reach the top of the mountain by being a slacker. This made her think of Pearce.

She passed the halfway point.

Her quiet teammate had missed the last two practices. Miss Helen had said nothing to the other girls except, "We'll have to make do without her tonight." But Kaylee could tell from the look in her teacher's eyes that she was concerned. *Nice to have her focused on somebody else's shortcomings for a change.*

However, Kaylee also felt anger toward Pearce. The other girls on the oireachtas team seemed to have become more focused in the past week. Even Joleen had stopped complaining and seemed excited about the group's chances. But Pearce never showed any emotion, never seemed excited about the prospect of going to the Midwest Championships, and now she was starting to miss workouts.

"She's weird," said Joleen after one practice. "It's like having a cat on the team. It never makes a sound and just stares at you with those big eyes."

Kaylee passed the two-mile mark, where Elk Horn Road turned off to the right.

"I wish she'd talk more," said April. "Maybe she feels intimidated because she's only thirteen and most of us on the ceili team are fourteen."

Gina had shrugged. "I'm thirteen. It doesn't bother me."

Then yesterday, when Pearce had showed up for practice, she had turned the wrong way in the middle of Trip to the Cottage. And she had done it twice. Miss Helen had, of course, admonished her, but Kaylee felt Pearce deserved a much sharper rebuke than what Miss Helen had offered. And she had delivered it after class.

As Pearce had laced on her street shoes—sitting off by herself, as usual—Kaylee had slid next to her.

"We're a good team," Kaylee had said, trying to sound diplomatic. "We've got a chance to recall. But you can't be missing practices. What if you turned the wrong way at oireachtas?"

Pearce seemed neither ashamed nor combative. She simply stared back at Kaylee as if tolerating this nuisance.

Two and a half miles.

"Don't you care how we do?" Kaylee pressed Pearce.

Suddenly Miss Helen's voice rang out behind her. "Kaylee, that will do!"

Kaylee whirled around to see that her teacher had come up from behind and now she dismissed Pearce with a wave. Turning back toward Miss Helen, Kaylee felt her temper building.

"But—"

Miss Helen momentarily silenced her with a shake of her head. "No buts."

Kaylee plunged ahead anyway. "She's skipping practices! She's making mistakes! You've always said we have to work hard to—"

Again Miss Helen cut her off. "It is not your place to discipline your teammates. If something needs to be said, a teacher will say it."

Kaylee felt her mouth drop open, recalling the modest rebuke that Pearce had suffered in practice. "But you let her off easy."

Miss Helen's gaze was steady. "That is your opinion."

"It's a fact!" Kaylee's voice grew louder. "If I had missed team practices and goofed up my steps, you would have treated me like a criminal!"

"Kaylee!"

"You would have lectured me about hard work and teamwork and made me feel like a lazy slacker and a quitter!" She could not stop herself. "Well, I'm not those things! I'm not Lizzie Martin!"

"That is enough!" Kaylee had never heard Miss Helen shout before. She had always ruled the classroom with a resolute sternness that had never required her to raise her voice except to be heard above the music. This outburst had the effect of a thunderbolt and turned all heads toward Kaylee and her teacher. It also seemed to have cost Miss Helen something, for while as resolute as usual, the color seemed to have drained from her face. After a moment, she turned and walked slowly toward the office.

Now Kaylee could feel the eyes of other dancers, incredulous eyes fixed onto the girl who had made Miss Helen shout. She had quickly slipped off her ghillies, grabbed her duffel bag and run to her mother's car in stocking feet.

She spotted the rock piles and the Grant Farms sign, turned down the gravel drive, picking up the pace in the process. She felt the friendly burning in her lungs.

Although every dancer at Trean Gaoth Academy learned of Miss Helen's history, no one had ever spoken to her about Lizzie Martin. Everyone seemed to understand the hurt this had caused the old woman and had respected the bit of folklore enough to confine discussions of it to secret occasions.

Everyone except Kaylee.

Kaylee had gone home that evening, had sat at the desk in her room and opened the center drawer. A clutter of pencils, pens, a bracelet and a couple of gum wrappers lay atop a battered school folder marked MATH. She removed the folder, which had nothing to do with school. By writing the word MATH on the cover, Kaylee had guessed that Will would have no interest in it should he ever decide to go poking through her desk. That was probably true for her parents as well. Opening the folder, a math worksheet stared at her from the pockets on either side. These were decoys as well, placed there to complete the ruse.

In this folder were Kaylee's most personal and valuable possessions. And one of these was the letter from Lizzie Martin.

Two years ago, Kaylee had discovered the letter by accident in a box of old papers in her mother's office at the Stitchin' Kitchen.

Hey,

Thanks for inviting me for pizza with you and the gang, but I can't on Friday. Big soccer game. What can I say? It's my life! We'll do the pizza some other time!

Lizzie Martin

The letter proved that her mother had known Lizzie Martin in college. It had also helped explain why Miss Helen had always hated Kaylee. Somehow, the old woman had discovered this connection. Clearly, any friend of Lizzie Martin's was an enemy to Miss Helen. As a result, she had worked Kaylee harder than any of the other dancers.

Kaylee had asked her mother about Lizzie Martin, but Mrs. O'Shay had not offered much information. Yes, her mother admitted, Lizzie had been an incredible dancer. But Kaylee had gotten the impression that some unpleasant circumstance had driven apart Lizzie and her mother years ago.

She removed the worksheet tucked into the left pocket. Behind it was a photograph that she had inherited from her aunt. Kaylee felt her throat tighten as she stared at the picture of Aunt Kat, a senior in high school in her track uniform, her arm around her sister, who was, of course, Kaylee's mother. The two young girls smiled out at the world, one of them unaware that her choice in friends would one day cause her daughter to be tortured by a dance instructor, the other unaware that her life was already half over.

Behind the photograph was another prize: the thick booklet from Kaylee's first feis. Tucked into this was a picture of Kaylee and Caitlin that Mrs. Hubbard had taken. How young they seemed to Kaylee.

Kaylee replaced those items as well as the worksheet. Then she removed the second math paper from the right pocket. A paper clip held a ticket stub in place, a memento of the ferry ride to the feis in Muskegon. She had stood on the top deck of the ferry with Riley. There was also a ribbon from the Paavo Hospital run to benefit cancer research.

The big item in the right pocket, however, was Aunt Kat's sketch book. It contained drawings from Aunt Kat's college days as well as dozens of recent renderings of dancers at last summer's feiseanna. Kaylee's favorite sketch, though, was a drawing imagining what Kaylee herself would look like in a beautiful green solo dress— just the kind that Kaylee really wanted.

But Kaylee paused at that sketch only a moment. She kept the letter from Lizzie Martin tucked into the sketch book, and this was what she wanted. She thumbed through the pages. When she reached the end, Kaylee realized that she had gone too fast and had missed the letter. She tried again.

Nothing.

A stab of panic flashed through her. *I always put the letter back in the sketchbook.*

Now she took everything out of the folder. She examined the feis program page by page just in case she had accidentally put the letter in the wrong place.

Still nothing.

It's got to be here!

But it wasn't. Even a search of the drawer turned up nothing.

It was impossible, Kaylee decided. There was no way she would have misplaced the letter. The only explanation seemed to be that someone had gone into her desk and taken the letter on purpose.

But why would anyone do that? It was simply an old letter. Her mother already knew about it. So did her father. It didn't make sense.

Kaylee was at a full sprint now, racing toward the turnaround, the smell of the farm strong in her nostrils. She slowed to a stop at the circle and rested her hands on her hips, drawing in deep breaths.

She remembered how Will had popped into her mind. Would he have taken something from her room? She remembered that he had once "borrowed" a Kennedy Park Middle School sweatshirt from her closet, and this sent her up the stairs in a rage.

It has to be Will! Nothing else makes any sense!

She burst into his room. Will sat on the floor in front of a prehistoric television set, his fingers traveling maniacally across a control pad in his hands, orchestrating movement and explosions on the screen. He took no more notice than if she had been a mosquito.

"What were you doing in my room?"

Will answered without taking his eyes from the battle. "I wasn't in your room."

"Yes you were," said Kaylee hoarsely. "You were in my desk! Something's missing!"

"I never go in your room," Will insisted. "It smells funny."

"You took my Kennedy Park sweatshirt!"

"That was just one time," said Will, glancing toward her for an instant. "I was cold. My sweatshirt was in the wash."

Kaylee felt as if she might scream. "Stop lying! Give me that letter, you little creep!"

Will's face became a pretzel of confusion. "What letter?"

Struggling for the harshest words in her vocabulary, Kaylee's eyes scanned the room, falling ultimately on a thin, plastic case containing one of Will's video games. She grabbed it and stepped back toward the doorway.

"Hey! I need that!"

Kaylee's eyes blazed with anger as she held the case aloft. "You'll get it when I get my letter back!"

Will took his eyes away from the screen, stood up and muttered an obscenity. "I didn't do anything!"

"Liar!"

Then Tom O'Shay had been behind her in the doorway. "What's going on?"

Kaylee knew she was defeated. "Nothing." She tossed the case onto the floor at her brother's feet, whirled and exited the room. As she started down the stairs, she heard her brother's explanation to their father.

"She thinks I stole some stupid love letter she got from a boy at school."

He has no idea. He really didn't take the letter.

An apology at this moment would have been embarrassing and awkward, and besides, Will *had* sworn at her and she was angry with him just on general principles. But if Will were innocent, then there was no reason anyone living in her house would take the letter. And she could think of no reason a burglar would ignore things like televisions and furniture, yet steal an old letter from a math folder in her desk. Ideas stormed through her brain, making Kaylee feel agitated and even angry, for it was all so utterly mad.

Now she stood erect and the sight of the red barn in front of her filled her with the hope that she might be able to forget the letter and the impossible circumstances surrounding its disappearance by immersing herself in her work at the farm.

She hoped they had a hard day planned for her.

Eight

"You'll probably place first in the two dances you need today," Caitlin had said as they arrived at the Chicago hotel for the feis. "Then you'll be in PC." She smiled, a bit sadly, Kaylee thought, but then added, "And you deserve it. You've been working so hard."

As she moved across the stage, performing her slip jig, she did not feel like she deserved it. Something was not right.

She focused. *Concentrate.*

Was it the arms? Were they straight enough? Her toes? Were they pointed out? The kicks? High enough? Was her knee locked? Posture? Facial expression? Everything had to be right. Was she hitting the beat? Did she seem graceful? Had she messed up on any of the complicated steps? Was she holding her leaps? The best dancers seemed suspended in air. Did she project confidence? Was her costume in order? No droopy socks, dog-eared competitor number or unfastened loop on her cape. Was her wig slipping? No, it seemed to be pinned tightly in place—so much so that the top of her head ached. And when she put all of those pieces of the puzzle together, did they add up to exactly what the judge was looking for on this particular day?

You're fine, she told herself. *You're doing great.*

Yet, something in her head played a contradictory tune. She felt that her troubled state of mind might have something to do with last night's dream.

Dreaming about Irish dance was not a new phenomenon. Half a dozen times she had found herself at a feis, usually at a hotel, and the outer hallways were always filled with people. She would be looking for her stage, and would travel down several twisting corridors until she finally emerged in a ballroom. But there would be no stage. No people, either. Just an empty room. When she would return to the hallway, it would be empty, too, as if everyone had suddenly left, or perhaps she had stumbled into the wrong hotel. As she searched frantically, she would usually wake.

"That's an anxiety dream," her mother had told her. "It just means you're nervous about the dance competition."

Last night's dream had been a bit different, and she had not shared it with her mother. It had been set in a hotel again, and when she arrived at the ballroom this time, it had been filled with people. She realized that she was wearing the beautiful green solo dress of her dreams. As she approached the stage, Caitlin came up beside her and cheered, "Good luck, Lizzie!" She stepped into the middle of the stage. Riley and Jackie and even Brittany Hall were in the crowd, smiling at her, chanting, "Lizzie! Lizzie!" And Aunt Kat was there, her face kind and beautiful. "Good luck, Lizzie!" Everyone quieted for the start of the music, but there was only silence. Then, as Kaylee looked out across the room, she noticed that it was empty and dark, and she stood there all alone.

The dream had torn at her. On one hand, it had scared her—the sudden darkness, the strangeness of people she knew calling her Lizzie Martin. Was that how she viewed herself? Deep inside, did Kaylee imagine that she was a talented dancer who, one day, would let everyone down? Or did the dream mean something else? Or nothing at all?

And on the other hand, she had wanted to go back to sleep in the hope that she might be able to repeat the dream. She had not dreamed of Aunt Kat since her death, and in her dream, her aunt had seemed so real. The pain of loss and residual grief had burned inside of her.

Now the slip jig drifted toward its conclusion. Kaylee pointed, bowed, returned to her place in the line. An hour later, the slip jig posting showed Caitlin in second. Kaylee's name was not listed.

So much for Caitlin's prediction.

The dream continued to bother her, and so did the mystery of the Lizzie Martin letter. A part of Kaylee realized that the dream was probably an understandable result of two things which had been on her mind a great deal lately. Hardly an hour went by that she did not puzzle over the lost Lizzie Martin letter. And, of course, Irish dance found ways to link itself to at least half of her conscious thoughts and ninety-five percent of her daydreams. So she had dreamed a crazy dream that combined the two concerns. Unfortunately, taking this rational approach did no more good than trying to convince oneself that ghosts did not exist while walking through a cemetery at midnight on Halloween.

The letter was the more bothersome of her concerns. She went over it again in her mind. The matter preoccupied her so thoroughly that halfway through the feis, Caitlin pulled her into a quiet area and voiced her concerns over a boat of nachos they had purchased at the concession stand.

"You've been really weird today," she said in a way that only best friends can. "What's wrong?"

Kaylee told her about the letter and was surprised at the amount of relief this seemed to bring. She had previously told Caitlin about the letter, but this new wrinkle concerning a possible theft fascinated her friend.

"It's driving me crazy. My parents are in the clear, since they both knew about the letter."

"Maybe Will was looking for money," suggested Caitlin.

Kaylee grudgingly shook her head. "He wouldn't do that. Besides, all my money's in a ceramic bank on my desk."

"Maybe he was playing a prank. You know, trying to take something that would make you mad."

Kaylee remembered her false accusations and the fight with Will. "I've pretty much eliminated my brother as a suspect. Besides, he would have taken one of my medals or my *Isle of Green Fire* movie or the stuffed bear I got from Hannah and Jordi at my thirteenth birthday party if he wanted to make me angry. When I mentioned the letter, he thought it was from a boy at school."

Caitlin bit off the corner of a chip and chewed for a moment before answering. "Maybe Will is a good actor."

Kaylee did not buy it. But if neither her parents nor Will was to blame, then who? Who else had access to her room?

"Could your grandmother have taken it?" asked Caitlin.

"I doubt it," replied Kaylee, noticing that she still held the first chip she had picked up at the start of their discussion. She popped it into her mouth and chewed. "She never comes into my room. I think it scares her a little, especially since I tore out the carpet and put up that poster of Angelo Zizzo without a shirt on that Jackie gave me. And why would she care about a letter my mom got in college? All it says is that Lizzie can't go out for pizza. It's not a formula for rocket fuel or a treasure map!"

Caitlin finished a couple more chips as she considered the matter. "When was the last time you saw the letter?"

Kaylee's brow furrowed. "Less than a week. I took out my secret folder to look at my aunt's sketch book. I do that a lot." Caitlin nodded sagely. "I saw the letter then. After that, I put the folder back in my desk drawer."

"And you've looked through the drawer?" asked Caitlin. "And on the floor under the desk, just in case?"

"Of course," replied Kaylee.

"What about kids from your school?" asked Caitlin.

Kaylee almost laughed. "What are you saying? That Brittany Hall broke into my house and stole the letter?" Although she had meant the statement to sound ridiculous, hearing it out loud sent a shiver up her vertebrae.

"What about Jackie?" Caitlin asked. "She wouldn't have taken it for some reason, would she?"

It was true that Jackie knew about the letter and that her overzealous—although often well-intentioned— schemes had sometimes gotten her into trouble. However, Kaylee explained that Jackie had not been at the O'Shay home for almost two weeks.

Caitlin shook her head in frustration, walking the chip boat—which she had emptied with little assistance—to a garbage can. "I'm out of ideas." Then she turned back toward Kaylee. "Your house isn't haunted, is it?"

Kaylee sighed. "Not that I've noticed. Unless my creepy thirteen-year-old brother counts."

She had hoped that talking over the mystery with Caitlin might help her see something that she had missed. Maybe there were other possibilities that were more likely than what she had been able to figure out on her own. But while it had been nice to share her angst with Caitlin, their inability to come up with tangible explanations for what had happened to the letter had not diminished it.

As they wandered in the general direction of their camp, the two girls found themselves near the stage where the Preliminary Championships were contested. "That'll be us someday," said Caitlin, pointing.

Kaylee watched with glazed eyes for a few moments. When she pushed away the swirl of anxious thoughts that had made focus so difficult, she noticed that she and Caitlin were watching girls their own age. Kaylee grimaced, knowing that this probably meant Brittany Hall would be up there. Brittany had already won a PC competition and only needed one more win to move to the highest level of all: Champion.

But as Kaylee strained to see over the people seated in chairs in front of the stage, she could not spot Brittany's gorgeous emerald-green dress. It was exactly the color and style that Kaylee had always wanted for herself, and she felt a deep longing every time she watched Brittany dance in it.

Caitlin pointed suddenly. "There's Little Miss Evil Incarnate."

Kaylee squinted, seeing no green. But then she saw red.

"She's got a new dress!" cried Kaylee. "What the heck! The green one couldn't have been half a year old!"

The gorgeous, apple-red gown shimmered. Five white panels on the front rested above puffs of white tuili. "It's amazing," said Caitlin, and Kaylee had to admit she was right. She seethed as she watched her smiling nemesis waiting her turn to perform. Brittany Hall had money. She could get a new dress anytime she wanted. It just wasn't fair.

When Kaylee checked the results posters at the end of the day, she felt even worse. She had placed only in her hornpipe, and that had been a fifth. *So much for being on the fast track to PC.*

Caitlin had earned two second place finishes and one third. She was a little disappointed, since she had hoped to gain a first in at least one of her dances. However, she did not complain a bit, knowing that her best friend felt far worse.

"I don't understand it," said Kaylee morosely as they rode home in the Hubbard van. "I've been working so hard! I've been running more! I've been practicing more at home! And this is one of the worst feises I've ever had!"

Caitlin offered a tepid smile. "Don't take it too hard. You know how judges can be. Besides, you've already got two first places."

Kaylee did her best to control herself. She knew that if she spoke she would say something mean-spirited. Didn't Caitlin understand that those two first place finishes didn't mean anything unless she got the other two? Since she was an Irish dancer, she certainly should have understood this and also how important it was to Kaylee. Kaylee felt that her ability to remain quiet ranked as perhaps her most impressive athletic accomplishment of the day.

The Hubbards dropped Kaylee off at her home just before six. The sun still hung hours above the horizon. "How'd you do?" asked her mother, seated at the table, as Kaylee banged through the kitchen entrance. It took only one glance at her daughter's face to know the answer. Mrs. O'Shay decided that it might be better to save additional interrogation for a sunnier moment, and so she went back to balancing the family checkbook. A few minutes later, Kaylee emerged from her room wearing shorts and a t-shirt.

"I'm going for a run."

Mrs. O'Shay glanced at the clock. "Are you sure, sweetheart? It's getting late and you must be tired from the dancing and travel."

"The sun won't be down for hours," said Kaylee, who exited the way she had arrived. Outside, she took a deep breath of the Cranberry Street air and took off at a brisk pace. In the first quarter mile, tears trickled down her cheeks, but the summer breeze felt good, as did the exertion. Unlike with dance, a runner could *see* that she was making progress. She didn't have to guess or depend on some stupid judge's opinion.

She passed a couple of joggers heading in the other direction and soon found herself at the edge of town.

She kept going, fueled by hurt, disappointment, confusion, and waves of emotion she could not readily identify.

Before she knew it, her legs had carried her down the gravel driveway that led into Grant Farms. She did not stop at the house, but instead jogged down the incline, tiptoed gingerly through the corral and let herself into the stable. She petted each of the horses for a few moments and gave each a chunk of carrot. Each time her hand brushed against one of the animals, Chicago and the horrid feis seemed to recede even farther into the distance. Lizzie Martin seemed to become less important.

  She came to Trooper last, and as Kaylee stroked his mane, she leaned her small head against his big one.

  And Trooper let her.

Nine

"You are ready to be tested," announced Miss Helen after practice as the girls walked to their duffel bags lining the edge of the carpet. "There is a feis in Kenosha at the end of July where you will dance your ceili. It will be good to perform in front of a judge."

The girls exchanged anxious glances and a few smiles.

"You will also dance your ceili at the lakefront international festival in Milwaukee in August. Thousands of people will be watching, and so it will be a good way to learn to deal with any nervous issues."

Kaylee recalled dancing at World Fest last year. She had performed in a large group of about thirty dancers, and her stomach had still behaved as if she had swallowed hyperactive butterflies the size of raccoons. With a sea of people stretching away from the giant outdoor stage, she had felt like a rock star. Kaylee could only imagine what it might be like to dance in a small ceili group in front of thousands of eyes.

Miss Helen retrieved a pile of yellow handouts and distributed one to each girl. "This will give your parents all the information they need. Make sure you do not forget to give it to them. Pearce will get hers at the next practice."

Kaylee flashed a glance toward Miss Helen, who conveniently faced away from her. Pearce had missed another practice. This bothered Kaylee immensely, not only because of the deleterious effect she was certain it would have on their ceili team's chances of recalling at oireachtas, but also because of Miss Helen's mild reaction to this offense.

I would have been yelled at, kicked off the ceili team, and probably forced to watch as my dance shoes were fed into a leaf mulcher.

This convinced Kaylee even more that Miss Helen hated her because of her mother's long-ago friendship with Lizzie Martin. Although Miss Helen rarely played favorites, it was easy to see which dancer she was the hardest on.

On Friday evening, Kaylee hauled her sleeping bag and duffel into Jackie's room for a much-anticipated Fourth of July weekend sleepover. Incredibly, it was only their second sleepover of the summer, which had been filled with Jackie's soccer camps and Kaylee's dance and work on the farm. Tonight, the Kizobus were driving the girls to the fireworks show at Kennedy Park across from the middle school. The show was not as spectacular as the one in nearby Paavo. Still, Kaylee was glad they had opted to stay in Rosemary. Going to the Paavo show would only have reminded her of Aunt Kat, who had taken Will and Kaylee to the Fourth of July fireworks there last year.

As they spread their sleeping bags on the floor, Kaylee brought Jackie up to date on Pearce, Miss Helen and the letter.

"You're not thinking that old fossil snuck into your house and stole your Lizzie Martin letter, are you?" asked Jackie surreptitiously as she repositioned a small, framed photograph of Angelo Zizzo on her desk so that she would be able to see it from the floor.

The image of the old woman in her shabby, charcoal sweats climbing through a side window at the O'Shay house was enough to force a tiny smile from Kaylee.

"Maybe you should talk to your mom about Lizzie Martin," suggested Jackie.

"I've done that," said Kaylee. "A couple of times."

Jackie considered this as she fluffed and refluffed her pillow. "What has your mom told you about her?"

"Well," said Kaylee, searching her memory, "that they were friends in college. That Lizzie was a great dancer. And I guess that she hasn't seen her for a long time." She paused. "It seems like maybe something bad happened. Like an argument or something. I don't know for sure. My mom has never really wanted to say much about it."

Jackie's eyes went wide. "Maybe your mom and Lizzie both liked your dad! Maybe that's what destroyed her friendship with Lizzie!"

This thought had occurred to Kaylee last year, but it had seemed ridiculous—and still did. "My dad is old and losing his hair and . . . *dad*-like. No one's going to fight over him."

"Yeah," said Jackie, "but when he was younger, he probably looked more like Will."

Kaylee cast her friend a sideways glance. "You're starting to scare me. Besides, it wouldn't explain why Miss Helen hates me. Lizzie Martin must have been popular. But it wouldn't make sense for Miss Helen to hate all of the children of all of Lizzie's friends. It's almost as if . . ."

"What?" asked Jackie.

"I was just thinking." Kaylee tapped her fingers soundlessly on Jackie's carpeted floor. "For Miss Helen to hold that sort of grudge, you'd think my mom was responsible for Lizzie Martin quitting Irish dance. But that doesn't make any sense, either."

"Your mom could have been a soccer player," suggested Jackie. "And maybe she talked Lizzie into doing soccer rather than dance."

Kaylee laughed. "Trust me, my mom's not the athletic type."

She recalled the day that Aunt Kat had first showed her the photo of the two sisters taken after her aunt had won the 800-meter run. Kaylee had asked what event her mother had competed in.

"Oh, your mom didn't run track," Aunt Kat had said.

She had not done any school sports. Aunt Kat had been the athlete of the family. Her mother had been more inclined to sit in front of a sewing machine like Grandma Birdsall.

"Besides," added Kaylee, "Lizzie would have been in high school when she quit dance. My mom was friends with her in college."

Suddenly, Jackie slapped the floor with both palms. "We should track down Lizzie Martin!"

"What?"

"With the Internet, how hard could it be? If you could talk to her, I'll bet you could find out the answers to all of your questions! Maybe she lives in the area!"

The idea that she might actually talk to Lizzie Martin had seemed like an impossible dream to Kaylee. Lizzie had always been some wispy specter hidden in the mists of the family history, a bit of dark mythology like the bogeyman or Darth Vader. To actually come face-to-face with her and find the answers to her questions . . .

How did you meet my mother?

Why don't you talk to each other anymore?

Why did you quit dance when you were so close to the top of the mountain?

Did my mother do something that would make Miss Helen hate me?

And the most important question:

Do you wish you could go back and do it differently?

"If we were going to do it," Kaylee said slowly, "we'd have to do it at your house. My father only lets me use the computer for homework."

"That shouldn't be a problem," Jackie nodded gleefully. "I'm rather adept at duplicitous behavior."

Kaylee leaned back against her pillow and stared at the ceiling. "But where would we start? If we type LIZZIE MARTIN into a search engine, we'll probably come up with thousands of people who aren't the right one. And she could be married now! Her name might be Lizzie Gardelbardelopolous for all we know!"

Jackie looked stricken. "If that's her name, I can understand why your mother wants nothing to do with her. Even addressing a Christmas card would be painful."

On an impulse, Jackie moved to the laptop on her desk. She brought up the browser. "What college did you say your dad attended?"

Kaylee squinted, trying to recall the name on the videotape of his championship soccer game. "I think it was Northland. But will it be okay with your parents if we snoop around on your computer?"

"I'll see," said Jackie brightly. She moved to the doorway and called down the hall. "Mom?"

"Yes?" came Mrs. Kizobu's reply.

"Kaylee needs to do some research for Irish dance! Can we use the computer?"

"Of course, dear! But you've only got about fifteen minutes until we leave for the Fourth of July show!"

Jackie smiled at her friend and moved back to her desk. "You said Northland?" She typed this in and the hits piled up. She pointed to the top one. "Yes?"

Kaylee shook her head. "That one says it's in Minnesota. Dad went to school in Wisconsin."

Jackie scrolled down. "Here it is!" She clicked and the college home page popped onto the screen.

Northland College—home of the Fighting Nessies

"Oh Geez!" Kaylee stared at an image in the corner of the screen. "The mascot at my dad's school was the Loch Ness monster! I think I'm going to be ill!"

"But it's so cute!" said Jackie.

"He looks angry to me."

"You'd be angry, too, if people were constantly trying to take your picture or harpoon you."

"How's this going to help us find Lizzie Martin?" asked Kaylee, watching as Jackie found the site directory and clicked on ATHLETICS.

"I was just thinking," said Jackie, "that Lizzie's college soccer coach might still be there. We could call her and see if she knows where Lizzie lives!"

"Do you think she'd give out information like that on the phone?"

Jackie shrugged as **NORTHLAND COLLEGE ATHLETICS** appeared at the top of the screen. "She might give us the town. That would put us closer than we are now. You could tell her that your dad is trying to track Lizzie down for some kind of reunion. How long ago did your dad and mom graduate?"

"I think it was something like right when I was born," said Kaylee.

"Ah," said Jackie, intent on the screen. "Women's Soccer. And there's a picture of the coach. It says, 'Northland has enjoyed a long tradition of success in women's soccer. Its current coach, Marilyn Sanders, has led the team to winning seasons in six of her nine years at the helm."

Jackie sighed. "Nine years. So she wouldn't have coached Lizzie Martin."

An idea occurred to Kaylee. "Check out the men's coach."

"That's good," said Jackie, catching on immediately and tapping away at the keyboard. "Maybe he's been there long enough to remember her!" Her face lit up as she read his bio. "Twenty-seven years! Jack Warren. He might remember her. Let's give him a call!"

A chill ran through Kaylee. Playing detective had been amusing, but the idea that they might now have to follow through and actually confront the past frightened her. Then she remembered the day and time. "It's Friday night! The coach isn't going to be in his office!"

Jackie's fingers tapped rapidly. "Who said we were going to call his office? Unless he's got an unlisted number, we can look it up online!"

My parents are right, thought Kaylee. *The Internet is dangerous.*

In a minute, Jackie had the number. She dug out her cell phone and handed it to Kaylee.

Kaylee shrunk back. "I can't do this!"

"Sure you can," said Jackie. "Just sound pleasant and mention your dad's name. Coaches love to hear from former athletes. Especially the good ones."

Kaylee took a deep breath. After all, she had been wanting to find answers about Lizzie Martin. Now, she might be on her way to getting them. She dialed the number Jackie indicated on the screen.

Maybe he won't be home, she hoped.

"Hello?"

Kaylee cleared her throat. "Is this Mr. Warren?"

"Yes it is," said the man.

"The soccer coach?"

"Yes, this is Coach Warren."

Kaylee's mind suddenly went blank.

"Hello?" asked Coach Warren. "Who is this?"

Jackie waved her arms frantically and Kaylee remembered what she wanted to say. "I-I'm sorry to call you at home, sir. My name is Kaylee O'Shay." Pause. "My father is Tom O'Shay."

Now there was a pause on the other end. "For goodness sake! Why, I haven't seen Tom in years! And you're his daughter, you say?"

"Yes sir."

"Well, this is a surprise!" Then the coach's voice became serious. "Say, I hope you're not calling with bad news. Tom's all right, I hope."

"Oh, yes," said Kaylee. "He's fine."

"One of the best forwards I ever coached," said Coach Warren. "What's Tom doing these days?"

"He works at Rosemary High School."

"I remember Tom wanted to be a history teacher," said Coach Warren.

"He actually works in maintenance," said Kaylee.

"I see," said the coach. "Well, what can I do for you, young lady?"

Kaylee could hardly control her voice. "I was wondering if you remember an athlete from the women's team. Lizzie Martin?"

Coach Warren laughed. "Of course I remember Lizzie! She was a heck of a player, too!"

She breathed a bit easier. Maybe this wouldn't be as difficult as she had imagined.

"Well, what I'm wondering, sir, is whether you know where Lizzie Martin is living today."

The silence surprised her. At first, Kaylee wondered whether Jackie's phone had dropped the call. After a few moments, she realized that the coach was still on the line. He just wasn't answering. Finally, in a much more serious voice, he said:

"What do you mean?"

Kaylee's voice began to shake a bit. "Like, I was just thinking that maybe you knew the town. Or something. You see, Lizzie used to be a good friend of my mother."

Again there was an uncomfortably long silence. Jackie's eyes were wide, curious. When Coach Warren spoke again his voice was gravely serious.

"What did you say your name was, young lady?"

Kaylee wanted to hang up, but she mustered her courage and said, "Kaylee, sir."

"And you're really Tom O'Shay's daughter?"

"Yes sir."

"Holy cow!" Coach Warren cleared his throat. "I think, young lady, that this is a question that you'll need to take up with your parents."

Then the line went silent. She handed the phone back to Jackie.

"What'd he say?" asked her friend, who had noticed how white Kaylee's face had become.

"He said he couldn't tell me anything," said Kaylee. "But it was the way he said it. As if I had asked a question that shouldn't have been asked." She grabbed Caitlin's hand, and her friend almost recoiled from the icy touch. "I think whatever happened between Lizzie and my mom is a lot worse that we thought—and I'm scared!"

At that moment, Mrs. Kizobu called down the hall.

"Let's go girls! The fireworks are about to start!"

Ten

She fed the horses, brushed them, shoveled out their stalls. She climbed the wooden ladder into the upper barn, dragged a bale from the pile and dropped it down a hole in the floor. Then she slid back down to the stable and spread straw at their hooves.

"Let's get you some exercise," Kaylee said to all of them, sliding back the bolt and throwing open the double-wide doors. Sun and fresh air poured in, and the horses shifted and grunted in anticipation.

She sent Whiskey out first, followed by Star and Seeley. Star sauntered immediately to the fence and stood there. Seeley trotted to the far gate and waited. Whiskey followed Seeley. Thunder took a few steps out from the barn and stood there as if not wanting to be hurried. Last came Trooper, who ran circles around the corral and brayed.

"I hear you," said Kaylee good-naturedly. "I'm coming. I'll get that silly gate and then you can run your hearts out in the pasture."

Kaylee jogged across the corral and pulled up the latch. Four horses cantered through the opening and spread out, at varying paces, into the pasture. Only Trooper remained in the corral.

Kaylee smiled. "Trooper, you're such a tease." She turned away from the gate, pretending that she wasn't watching. Finally, Trooper made his way to the opening and, just before racing through, gave Kaylee a nudge.

Kaylee whirled and gave Trooper a pat on the flank as he passed. She watched them frolic for a few minutes before turning back to the corral—and the shovel.

An hour before noon, Bob appeared at the corral and watched Kaylee work for a moment before approaching.

"You're a hard worker," he said as he lumbered toward her. "You've got a lot of heart. I think if I told you to tear down the barn and rebuild it a hundred feet to the north, you'd find a way to do it."

Kaylee looked at him uncertainly. "You weren't thinking of doing that, were you?"

Bob grunted a miserable pebble of laughter. "Kaylee, you're one of a kind. And you're good with the horses. Even Trooper seems to like you. In fact, I'd say you're about the only one Trooper does like."

Kaylee's eyes traveled to the pasture. "Trooper's one of a kind, too."

"I was thinking," Bob continued. "You've been working about twenty hours a week. Maybe you'd like to go full-time the rest of the summer. And in the fall, after school starts, you could work a few hours each night, taking care of the horses. You'd be putting away some pretty good money."

Pretty good money! In the few weeks Kaylee had already worked at Grant Farms, she had saved almost half the cost of her new school dress—after subtracting the expense of a few clothing items she had purchased as a treat for herself at the Cream City Mall. It felt good knowing that she was earning the dress herself, that her parents would not be burdened by the cost. It felt good knowing, for once, that money was not a problem. Still, forty hours a week would be a big change. She would have fewer hours of free time—fewer hours to spend with Jackie and her other friends.

And fewer hours to practice Irish dance.

On the other hand, she wasted a good deal of the afternoon as it was, just sitting around listening to music or watching TV or riding her bike.

And the O'Shays could always use more money.

"Thanks," Kaylee said politely. "I'll talk it over with my parents."

The word "parents" brought with it the first gloomy thought she had entertained in three hours. Her work at the farm had happily preoccupied her, driving out thoughts of Pearce, Brittany Hall, Kaylee's lackluster performance at the last feis, even her Aunt Kat. Now she was reminded of the questions she knew she had to ask her mother.

In her mind, she had replayed the telephone conversation with Coach Warren dozens of times. Why had his tone changed so abruptly? One moment they had been chatting away like old friends. And then, it had been as if some barrier had come between them—a barrier that Coach Warren had been unwilling to cross. He had not seemed to mind when Kaylee mentioned Lizzie Martin's name. But when she had asked where Lizzie Martin was, his cordiality had evaporated and he had quickly steered the conversation to an end.

I think, young lady, that this is a question that you'll need to take up with your parents.

Kaylee thought about this statement as she rode home with Mrs. Grant. "You're awful quiet today," said the older woman.

Kaylee smiled. "Just tired, I guess." In truth, now that she was no longer preoccupied by her farm chores, the unresolved Lizzie Martin questions pushed all other business from her mind. Coach Warren had implied that her parents knew something that he could not—or would not—discuss with her. But what?

When she arrived home, she cleaned up and tried to watch *Isle of Green Fire*, but even this was no good, and she stopped the movie after only a few minutes. As she sat on the edge of her bed, looking at—but not really seeing—the gleaming awards that littered the top of her dresser, a sudden inspiration hit her.

Maybe I should talk to Grandma Birdsall about Lizzie Martin.

She hopped off her bed and moved swiftly into the hall. She had previously avoided broaching the subject with her grandmother. After all, Grandma Birdsall had not gone to college with her daughter. How much would she really know about Bethany O'Shay's friends?

After the conversation with Coach Warren, however, Kaylee was more apprehensive than ever about talking with her mother. But perhaps Grandma Birdsall knew enough about Lizzie Martin to give Kaylee some sort of clue. Then perhaps Kaylee would feel more comfortable talking to her own mother, would know which questions she should ask.

Kaylee approached her grandmother's room and found the old woman awake. Because of her heart ailment and the stew of medicine she consumed every morning, Grandma Birdsall often napped away most of the afternoon. Today, however, she sat in a small, padded chair, stitching away at some dark material.

"Well, how's my beautiful granddaughter?" Grandma Birdsall held her arms wide, and Kaylee bent to gratefully accept the hug. "You didn't come to sew with me, did you?"

Kaylee remembered how her grandmother had given her sewing lessons several years earlier. Although they had been fun, and Kaylee had enjoyed spending time with her grandmother, she had eventually made excuses to miss the Sunday afternoon instruction so that she could spend time with Jackie or other friends. The memory made her feel guilty. Yet, her grandmother never seemed to harbor any resentment nor waver in her love.

"I can sew for a little bit," said Kaylee, settling on the edge of her grandmother's immensely fluffy bed. This seemed to fill Grandma Birdsall's face with a light and vitality that Kaylee had not seem in months. She looked to a basket sitting beside her and pulled out a triangle of fabric from which a lacy bit of appliqué dangled.

"Use this needle," she said, handing the items to her granddaughter. "Stitch the appliqué onto the fabric. You can see where it has pulled loose."

Kaylee tried to concentrate on the task, but her mind was full of the questions she wanted to ask. After a few minutes, however, she began to relax. Her grandmother's humming, the sun streaming through her bedroom window, the real progress she began to make on her sewing—these combined to create a contentedness that she had not felt in the O'Shay home for many months. Instinctively, Kaylee's eyes went to her grandmother's dresser, where she found a photograph of a smiling Aunt

Kat. For the first time since her aunt's death, seeing her picture did not make Kaylee sad.

They sewed on. Occasionally there were questions from her grandmother about dance and the previous school year and her work at the farm. Then her grandmother would return to her humming.

Why did I ever stop letting Grandma Birdsall teach me to sew?

"You know," said her grandmother, after Kaylee had finished repairing the appliqué on a third triangle, "you seem in a much better mood than when you walked in here. Why, it looked like you were carrying the weight of the world on your shoulders."

Kaylee smiled. "Thanks, Grandma. This was just what I needed."

"Usually when a fourteen-year-old looks that serious, there's a boy involved," her grandmother said with a wink.

"Well," said Kaylee, figuring that the time had come to ask her questions, "it wasn't about a boy. I was wondering how well you knew Mom's friends when she was in college."

The way her eyebrows arched, Kaylee could tell that her grandmother had not expected the conversation to take this direction. "I knew some of them. Most were very nice. Sometimes your mother would even bring a friend home with her to spend the weekend." She smiled at these recollections.

Kaylee decided to plunge ahead. "Do you know what happened to Lizzie Martin?"

The smile vanished from her grandmother's face. She seemed to consider the question for a moment. "I think you should talk to your mother about Lizzie."

What's with this Lizzie chick? Kaylee wondered. *Whenever anybody asks a question about her, people act like I'm trying to steal government secrets.*

Kaylee nodded but offered one more question. "Grandma, do you know what happened to Lizzie?"

Grandma Birdsall took a long time to answer, and when she did so, it was with a reluctant nod. This made Kaylee's heart beat faster. Her question had an answer—and people who lived in the same house she lived in knew that answer.

An hour later, Kaylee returned to her room where she promptly fell asleep. Supper had passed when she finally woke to find her mother sitting beside her on the bed in the darkened room.

"You must have worked hard on the farm today," said Mrs. O'Shay mildly. "And I heard Grandma put you to work, too."

"I think we sewed for a couple of hours," said Kaylee, stretching onto her side and then, slowly, sitting beside her mother.

"She also said you were asking questions about Lizzie Martin," her mother continued seriously.

Kaylee brushed the hair away from her face and sighed deeply. "I don't know much about your friend. All I know is what I read in that old letter. She played soccer and liked pizza. And I know she danced for Golden and had Miss Helen for a teacher and quit even though she could have been a world champion."

Her mother made a sound in the dark as if she wanted to say something, but remained quiet.

"Like I said, I hardly know anything about her, but in some way, I feel like we're connected. You know what I mean? That if only I could meet her and ask her some questions, then everything would make sense."

This time, Mrs. O'Shay did speak. "I know you're looking for answers, sweetheart, but I think you should drop this obsession you have with Lizzie Martin. It can't lead anywhere good."

Kaylee groaned. "That's what everyone seems to say."

Her mother's voice reflected surprise. "Everyone?"

"Jackie and I decided to track Lizzie down." She described using the computer to get Coach Warren's number. As she spoke, she could feel her mother growing more tense beside her on the bed.

"What did Coach Warren tell you?" said Mrs. O'Shay tersely.

"That he couldn't tell me anything," said Kaylee, alarmed at her mother's change in demeanor. "That *you* would have to tell me about Lizzie Martin."

The quiet grew between them for a long time, although she no longer felt the same sense of tension radiating from her mother. Finally, Mrs. O'Shay spoke.

"You really want to know what became of Lizzie Martin?"

Kaylee nodded. Her mother slid closer, stroked Kaylee's hair for a few moments and then pulled her into a hug. When the hug finally ended, the two sat facing each other, their features barely discernible in the weak light coming from the hall. She felt as if she were in a dream, but this was real. She was about to find out whether Lizzie Martin lived in Rosemary, Milwaukee or China. She was going to learn whether Lizzie and her mother had parted ways because of a fight or whether other circumstances had taken them on different paths. She was about to learn why everybody had seemed reluctant to tell her any of these things.

Mrs. O'Shay spoke softly yet deliberately. "Lizzie Martin died a long time ago."

Kaylee drew in a sharp breath. This was not the answer she had expected. Somewhere inside of her she had always imagined she would one day sit face to face with Lizzie Martin and ask her all of the questions about Irish dance that she could never ask her mother. Now that day would never come, and knowing it made a part of her feel like crying.

"How long ago?"

"A little before you were born," replied Mrs. O'Shay.

So she and Lizzie Martin had never even existed in the same world.

"Why wouldn't Coach Warren tell me that? Or Grandma Birdsall?"

"It can be hard for children to hear about sensitive issues," said her mother. "They probably thought it would be better if I told you."

Kaylee sat quietly for a bit, but then asked, "How?"

Mrs. O'Shay sighed deeply, and for the first time, Kaylee realized how difficult this must be for her. "Car accident. One day she was a happy, talented soccer player, and just like that—"

Kaylee placed a hand on her mother's shoulder. "You must have been so sad."

Mrs. O'Shay pulled her daughter into a hug again. "I cried. Oh, you don't know how I cried."

Perhaps not, Kaylee thought. But she knew that her mother was crying now.

And then she realized that they both were.

Eleven

She fed the horses, brushed them, shoveled out the stalls and then waited for Amber, who arrived just as she had said she would. She was back at Grant Farms for only a couple of days before heading back to Minneapolis. Kaylee guessed that Amber missed the farm more than she had first let on.

"You do a better job than I ever did," said the older girl, her eyes sweeping the lower barn. "So . . . you'd like to try riding?"

Kaylee nodded eagerly.

"Have any particular horse in mind?"

"Trooper," said Kaylee, pointing.

Amber glanced at Kaylee as if she'd just plunked down a ridiculously high offer on the biggest lemon in the used car lot. "There's gentler choices for your first ride. You know what a pain Trooper is."

"Have you ridden Trooper?" asked Kaylee.

Amber nodded. "Sure. But I'm pretty stubborn. And Trooper knows it."

Kaylee licked her lips. "Well, then I'd like to ride him."

Amber headed toward the tack room, chuckling. "Looks like you're pretty stubborn, too."

After work, Kaylee rode to the Stitchin' Kitchen where she found her mother making coffee for a middle-aged woman with a dress pattern tucked beneath her arm. Another older woman roamed through the aisles of fabric bolts. Once the middle-aged woman received her coffee, she settled onto a stool and Kaylee had her mother to herself.

"And Trooper didn't hardly seem to mind that I rode him!" narrated Kaylee, excluding not even the tiniest detail. "Except that he nipped me when I first tried to mount. And then he threw his head around. But after that, it was like we had an understanding."

Mrs. O'Shay listened patiently. It took awhile, but her daughter's narration ultimately lost an infinitesimally small amount of steam, and the mother plunged in with a question.

"Do they still want you to work more hours?"

Kaylee nodded. "I haven't decided what I want to do yet. I don't want it to interfere with dance."

Mrs. O'Shay smiled lovingly at her daughter. "I know what you should do."

Kaylee's mouth dropped open slightly. "You do? I'll bet you think I should keep my hours just the way they are because you don't want me overdoing it."

This brought a soft laugh from her mother.

"Or," countered Kaylee, "maybe you think I should take the extra hours because it's good to not have to worry about money for a change!"

"Kaylee," said her mother, who took the young girl's hands in her own, "I was going to say that I think you should take some of your hard-earned money and reward yourself."

Kaylee blinked.

"Reward?"

"I know that the notion of money and reward don't often go together at the O'Shay house," said her mother wryly. "But you work so hard, sweetheart. And you've now earned just about enough for your new school dress. Whatever money you make after that is . . . well, it's yours! You can save it—and I hope you do that with at least some of it—or you can buy yourself something nice. Why don't you see if Jackie wants to go to a movie?"

When they had arrived, the Paavo movie theater had bustled like a freight yard attempting to ship a hundred tons of popcorn and sugar and sound in approximately ten minutes. Now, people proceeded more soberly through the lobby, some laughing, some looking for trash receptacles for empty popcorn buckets, some rolling their eyes at memories of the just-completed film—and two trying to balance soda straws on their noses.

"It's no use," said Kaylee, collapsing onto a padded chair near the wall. "I don't have the balance for it."

"Don't have the balance?" Jackie stood next to her, using both hands to straighten the straw as she stared skyward. "You're a dancer! If you don't have the balance, who does?"

Kaylee found a trash can at arm's length and deposited her straw. "Was that the funniest movie ever?"

The question seemed to give Jackie an excuse to end her attempt as well. "I know! When they were doing that thing with the mirror I thought I was going to wet myself!"

"Remind me to bring a towel to the next movie," said Kaylee. Jackie playfully punched her shoulder.

Kaylee checked her watch. "My mother won't be here for a few minutes. Let's check out the arcade."

The two skittered to the small games room that opened off of the lobby. There they found a game involving a spaceship that raced through an increasingly bizarre universe full of obstacles.

"You go first," said Kaylee, and Jackie stepped behind the controller, plugging her change into the machine. Kaylee watched Jackie weave around careening satellites for a bit and became dimly aware that a boy had taken a seat at the machine next to them. He began playing the cops-and-robbers shoot-em-up game, and Kaylee did her best to ignore him. Of course, when one is fourteen, it is almost impossible not to sneak just the tiniest little peek at a boy next to you—on the chance that he might just be cute.

Kaylee sneaked a peek.

The boy was cute.

In fact, the boy was Michael Black.

He gave no indication that he had noticed Kaylee, continuing to assassinate whoever appeared on the screen. Kaylee felt her palms begin to sweat, partly because it was Michael Black, the cutest boy in her grade at school, and partly because Brittany Hall usually wasn't far away.

"Out on a big date, I see, O'Shrimp!"

Kaylee turned halfway around now to see Brittany a short distance behind Michael. Jackie spoke up as soon as she heard the familiar voice.

"Actually, we're taking turns on this game, ridding the universe of vermin! Ah, I think I see your personal mother ship appearing on the horizon right now!"

Kaylee had planned on ignoring Brittany, but since Jackie had spoken, she could not resist asking a question that had been bothering her.

"What happened to your green dress?"

Brittany, wearing enough makeup to be mistaken for a twenty-five-year-old, squinted. "What?"

"You had a brand new red dress at the last feis," explained Kaylee. "But the green dress, it was . . . beautiful."

The compliment seemed to take the edge off of Brittany.

"Oh. Yeah, well, I just got tired of it. So my dad ordered the red dress. From Ireland, of course."

"What's going to happen to the old dress?"

Brittany shrugged. "I dunno. Probably let it rot in my closet." Then she eyed Kaylee warily. "Why are you so concerned about it?"

This was more difficult than Kaylee had imagined. It required her to swallow her pride, to overlook so many of Brittany's past sins, in order to get something she so desperately wanted.

"I was just wondering if you might be thinking of selling the old dress." It was perfect, of course. Now that Kaylee had a job, she could afford some nice things for herself. And the green dress was just the perfect shade. Even the design bore some resemblance to the Celtic knots on the dress that her Aunt Kat had drawn in the sketchbook. Although Brittany was a bit taller and broader, Kaylee was certain that her mother could manage the alterations.

Brittany's eyes seemed to bore right through Kaylee. "So you really like that dress?"

Kaylee nodded reluctantly.

"Why?" asked Brittany.

"Why are *you* so nosy?" called Jackie over her shoulder as she tumbled through the galaxy.

"It's okay," said Kaylee to her friend, and then refocusing her attention on Brittany. "I've always wanted a green dress. And my aunt drew a picture of me in a dress that looks kind of like yours."

This broke Brittany's stare. "Oh, yeah. Sorry about your aunt." She thought for a moment. "How much?"

Kaylee felt at a loss. "I really don't know what a dress like that is supposed to cost brand n—"

"No," said Brittany, "how much money do you have with you?"

Kaylee hesitated and then checked her pockets. "About $40."

Brittany held out her hand. "Deal."

Now Kaylee's eyes widened. "You can't be serious. It must have cost fifty times as much. Even if you give it to me for half price because it's used it would still—"

Brittany cut her off with a wave. "Look, I'm never going to wear it again, right? My old dresses are all just hanging in my closet. When I go off to college, my mom will probably have a bonfire. I figure I might as well get something out of it."

Kaylee's heart beat so forcefully she felt certain that a rib would crack.

"You're sure?"

Brittany nodded and Kaylee handed her the money.

"What just happened back there?" asked Jackie, not seeing the money exchange behind her back.

"I just bought a new solo dress," said Kaylee as her friend turned around.

Jackie scowled at Brittany. "If you bought it from her, I hope you got the extended warranty."

Michael's game ended at about the same time and he and Brittany turned to leave.

"When can I get the dress?" Kaylee called after them.

"I'll call you," said Brittany, and then she and Michael were gone.

Twelve

The new week became a racecar, shifting into a higher gear at each hairpin turn. When Kaylee did not hear from Brittany on Sunday or Monday, she decided to call her. After all, the next feis loomed less than two weeks away, and if Kaylee wanted to wear the green dress for her solo dances, she needed to give her mother time to make the alterations.

Of course, she also needed to find the right moment to actually tell her mother that she had purchased the dress, but she figured it would be easier to do this when she had the dress in her possession. Once her mother could see how beautiful it was and how perfect it would look on her daughter, she would probably forget the number of hours she was going to have to devote to the task.

Kaylee called the Hall residence three times on Tuesday, each time getting their answering machine.

"I wish I knew Brittany's cell number," said Kaylee to Jackie as she hung up after the third attempt. The two returned to eating cookies in the O'Shay kitchen.

"Don't say I didn't warn you," said Jackie.

"You didn't warn me," replied Kaylee.

"That's only because you sealed the deal behind my back while we were in the arcade," said Jackie. "But I would have warned you. And you should have had enough sense to warn yourself. This is like that story by Washington Irving that we read in English class last year, *The Devil and Tom Walker*."

"Because Brittany Hall is like the devil, and people should know better than to strike deals with the devil?" asked Kaylee.

"No, because your dad's name is *Tom*!" Jackie rolled her eyes. "*Of course* it's because Brittany Hall is like the devil. In fact, she's like the devil's super-evil girlfriend who even makes Satan feel miserable."

Kaylee, however, did not trust her friend's instincts on this subject. While Brittany Hall was a jerk most of the time, Kaylee had noticed a couple of breaches in her armor. For instance, the previous summer, she had reached out to Kaylee a few times. They had talked about Kaylee's sick aunt. She had invited Kaylee to a party. For the first time, Brittany had seemed approachable, even *human*.

And Brittany knew that Kaylee wanted to buy the green dress because it was like a dress that her aunt had drawn. Kaylee could tell that, despite her carefully manicured layers of toughness and bravado, Brittany understood how Kaylee felt.

Dance classes added to the week's anxiety load, too. Pearce even arrived on time, but she still seemed to make far too many errors for Kaylee's taste. Still, Kaylee bit her lip, not wishing to once again incur Miss Helen's wrath.

Finally, on Wednesday, Kaylee reached Brittany by phone. "About the dress," said Brittany. "I'm going to need more money. When I told my parents I was selling it, they jumped all over me about what an expensive dress it was and I couldn't just sell it for forty bucks."

Kaylee exhaled slowly. She had half expected something like this might occur once Brittany's parents found out she intended to peddle the costume. She hoped the price would not be too high.

"I need another $60."

Kaylee almost laughed. That would make $100 total, which was still an incredible deal for such a gorgeous dress.

"I'll be working tomorrow afternoon at my mom's shop," said Brittany. "You can bring it by then."

On Thursday after work, Kaylee biked to Aunt Victoria's Antiques, which stood directly across from the apartment building in which Kaylee's Aunt Kat had lived. Kaylee stared at the brick exterior, remembering the hours she had spent there, wondering who was living in her aunt's apartment now, knowing that it would never be as cheerful or as full of beautiful and creative things as when her aunt had lived there. She tried to push out of her mind the final images of her aunt in the hospital, of the role that Brittany Hall had played in losing the medal her aunt had won—Kat's greatest athletic achievement.

She entered Aunt Victoria's, causing a tiny bell on the door to jingle. The inside of the store contained old wooden furniture, items made from pewter and wrought iron, dishes and glassware, ornately framed mirrors, and much more. Everything smelled of dust and polish. At first the large main room seemed deserted, but then Kaylee noticed a middle-aged woman with electric-blonde hair and layers of shiny makeup slouched in an overstuffed chair about halfway to the back wall. Her mouth hung open and a soft buzzing sound escaped with her exhalations. Brittany had confessed that her mother drank often, and Kaylee had witnessed her intoxicated behavior on at least one occasion. It appeared to explain her current state.

"Hello?"

A few muffled bumps sounded from a doorway at the back of the room and Brittany appeared, her eyes squinting into the gloom and then widening in recognition. "Oh, hi."

Kaylee dug into her pocket and took out the rest of the money.

"Not here," said Brittany, lowering her voice slightly. "She needs to sleep it off. Let's go outside."

The two stepped onto the sidewalk where Kaylee offered the bills.

"Here's the rest of the money."

Brittany, who seemed more anxious than usual, pocketed the cash quickly.

"Look," she said, "there's a little problem."

Oh, no, thought Kaylee. *Don't let Jackie be right!*

"Isn't the dress here?"

"The dress is fine," Brittany assured her. "But it's still at my house. You see, there was a little misunderstanding."

Kaylee's eyes grew dark. "What do you mean?"

"Well, you remember how my parents said $40 was way too cheap for such a nice dress? I thought they said I could sell the dress for $100, but what they actually said was $200."

Kaylee felt herself becoming angry. Suddenly she wanted to punch Brittany Hall in the face. Even though it would probably mean that Brittany would then beat her into a lumpy mass of random O'Shay molecules, she could hardly control the urge. On the other hand, it was possible Brittany was telling the truth. It was even reasonable. $200 was still a magnificent deal. The dress was easily worth ten times as much, even secondhand. And Kaylee did not want to mess up the deal by allowing her temper to get the best of her.

"The price isn't going to keep going up, is it?" asked Kaylee, endeavoring to control her voice. "$300? Then $500? Then $1000?"

"No," said Brittany, shaking her head. "My parents are okay with this. Just come back here on Monday and I'll have the dress."

Kaylee felt like she had no choice. If she backed out now, would Brittany even return the money? She had not gotten a receipt, and both Michael and Jackie had been facing the other direction in the arcade. It would be her word against Brittany's.

The following day, she informed Bob Grant that she would be happy to work the extra hours he had offered. She figured she could use the additional money to cover the unexpected price tag on her new solo dress.

"You can start your new hours on Monday, if you want," Bob told her.

The one bit of good news the week offered Kaylee was the arrival of her new school dress. It was actually a secondhand dress that the previous owner had finally dropped off, but it fit nicely and showed very little wear. Kaylee tried it on and pronounced herself very satisfied, although a part of her felt heavy, knowing that this dress had not been sewn by her grandmother.

"Time to pay up!" said her mother, and Kaylee produced her little bank. When the money lay on the kitchen table, she was still a few dollars short.

"You'll have to owe me for the rest," said Mrs. O'Shay. "I thought you had saved enough to pay for the dress."

Kaylee shrugged and muttered something about the movie maybe costing more than she had anticipated. Her mother still knew nothing about the new dress.

Once Monday is here, and she sees that green dress on me, I'll be able to relax!

Monday, however, started out as anything but relaxing. She could tell it would be a scorcher on her morning run to Grant Farms. *Just my luck. The first day I work eight hours is the hottest day of the summer!* By quitting time, Kaylee felt dirty, exhausted and ready for bed. However, as soon as Mrs. Grant dropped her off at home, she refreshed herself with a shower, grabbed a cookie from the kitchen, and spent a bit of time assuring her grandmother that everything was wonderful in her life. Then she tore off on her bicycle toward Aunt Victoria's on the other side of Rosemary's downtown business district.

CLOSED. The sign showing through the front door of the antique shop seemed to mock her as cruelly as if it had been Brittany's own face.

No. She wouldn't do this. She couldn't!

Kaylee tried to persuade herself that there was some reasonable explanation. Perhaps Mrs. Hall had become ill and had closed the shop early. That actually made a lot of sense. But Kaylee was not willing to rely on her imagination. In a moment, she leapt on her bike again and was on her way to Oakton Heights, Brittany's exclusive neighborhood. The trip did not take long, though the sky had become dusky by the time she steered onto Killdeer Court. A few minutes later she rolled to a stop in front of the white colonial-style home where Brittany lived. Faux pillars and black shutters accented the front of the two-story mansion. As she sat there, spotlights popped on, bathing the front of the building in an eerie blue light.

The driveway lay empty, but the closed garage door suggested the possibility that Mrs. Hall's car might be inside. Given her history, she was probably asleep. Brittany had bragged the previous summer that her mother often passed out in the evening, leaving Brittany with the run of the house. Mr. Hall held down two jobs to keep his daughter in an endless supply of solo dresses and his wife in a mansion, and so he usually did not arrive home until late.

Kaylee rang the doorbell. No one arrived. She rang again. Still no response.

Maybe no one's home after all.

On a whim, Kaylee decided to circle around the outside of the garage to the back of the house. She found the same elaborately landscaped lawn around the small stone patio that she had seen last summer, as well as the path leading off to the nearby woods. At the end of this path was where Brittany and her pals had smoked cigarettes and chugged beers and who knew what else. Kaylee had held a can of beer, had been tempted to take a sip, but had dropped the can when the police arrived. Then she had sprinted deeper into the woods to escape.

Some of Brittany's friends had not been so fortunate. However, Brittany had somehow gotten off with no consequences whatsoever. That seemed to be some sort of law of nature in Brittany's world.

The smell of campfire smoke and the faint murmer of voices told Kaylee that her hunch had been right. Brittany and some friends were probably sitting at the party spot in the clearing right now. She had come too far to leave now without her dress, and so Kaylee marched resolutely toward the laughter.

Only five of them ringed the campfire. Each had what appeared to be a can of beer. Michael Black and Brittany sat together on a low, wooden bench. Heather Chandler sat on Brittany's other side atop a chunk of firewood, and a boy and girl that Kaylee did not recognize rested on large rocks. A cigarette dangled from the mouth of Unknown Boy. They seemed oblivious to her presence until Heather blurted an obscenity followed by, "It's O'Shrimp!"

Kaylee stepped forward immediately, addressing Brittany, ignoring the others. "I've got the rest."

It seemed to take Brittany a moment to catch on to the fact that this unexpected person had arrived at this wholly inappropriate place. "The rest?"

"You were supposed to meet me at Aunt Victoria's," said Kaylee, keeping her voice level.

Brittany attempted a cool smile. "Yeah, well that didn't work out. You can blame my ma."

Kaylee nodded. "That's why I'm here. I've got the rest of it."

Now Brittany understood what the "it" meant, and she slowly rose, stepping around the campfire toward Kaylee. "Man, you really want this dress, don't you?"

Kaylee said nothing but pulled the $100 from her pocket and pushed it into Brittany's hand. Brittany stared at it for a moment before sighing and starting up the path. "I'll go get it." She disappeared through the brush and

Kaylee turned back to the campfire. Michael gave her half a smile, but then returned his attention to the blaze in front of him.

"Wish we had some marshmallows, man," moaned Unknown Boy. The two girls eyed Kaylee as if she had mortally offended them by, for instance, criticizing the precise amount of eye makeup they wore. She wished she had followed Brittany to the house. She thought she might go now, rather than wither in the uncomfortable spotlight of their gazes. However, Heather spoke up:

"So, O'Shrimp, what do you think you're doing, coming here uninvited?"

Kaylee said nothing.

"You realize," continued Heather, "that you can't just go barging onto private property whenever you want something. Having losers at our campfire spoils the whole evening!"

Unknown Boy let out a protracted "Ooh!" Kaylee remained quiet.

Now Heather stood and moved around the fire pit toward Kaylee, who stepped off to the right side, almost behind where Unknown Boy sat.

"Are you disrespecting me, O'Shrimp?" said Heather, her voice resonating hatred. "I talk to you and you just stand there like I'm nothing? You think you're better than all of us?"

This was going badly, as far as Kaylee was concerned. If not for the dress, she might have considered sprinting into the woods, disappearing the way she had a year ago. She felt a surge of relief when movement caught her eye and she spotted Brittany returning along the path—with the green solo dress dangling from a hanger. She stopped when she reached Heather.

"What's this?" said Heather, her eyes racing back and forth between Kaylee and the dress.

"You've seen this before," Brittany told her friend. "Kaylee wants my old solo dress."

Heather looked at Brittany. "How much she give you for it?"

Brittany shrugged. "Not much. I almost gave it away. O'Shrimp's parents aren't exactly millionaires. It's kind of like charity work."

The two boys laughed. Kaylee felt herself growing more angry and embarrassed. She took a step toward Brittany but froze when Heather reached out for the dress.

"Let me see it!"

Brittany looked toward Kaylee as if for guidance, beaming a wide yet clueless smile. Kaylee's face was as rigid as the statue of a frightened Irish dancer.

"What do you say, O'Shrimp?" asked Heather. "Can I look at the pretty dress? Or are you afraid I'll hurt your little baby?"

Kaylee was horrifically afraid. Her heart pounded as if the dress were indeed a tiny child, afraid that Heather, who had always had a special penchant for cruelty, might cast it into the fire. But for reasons she could not have described, she did not wish to show this fear to Heather or Brittany. And was even Heather so twisted that she would do such a thing?

"Let her look at the pretty dress!" moaned Unknown Boy, and Michael and the other girl joined in. Reluctantly, Kaylee nodded.

Heather took the hanger and supported the middle of the dress with her other hand. She showed it to the sitting three who oohed and ahed as if watching fireworks.

"You really wear stuff like that?" asked the other girl.

"That's cool," said Unknown Boy, although Kaylee suspected he would have said this if he had been shown a rock.

Kaylee took a step forward as Heather dipped the dress toward them, and Heather noticed this. Her smile widened. "Afraid I'll toss your dress in the fire, O'Shrimp?" She faked a little movement toward the blaze and Kaylee lurched involuntarily.

"Ooh! She is afraid!" Heather faked the movement a couple more times, her smile dissolving into a laugh. Finally, Kaylee could take it no more.

"Please!" she pleaded.

Brittany gave Heather a conciliatory shrug, and Heather transferred the hanger loop to her outstretched hand. However, Heather merely released the bottom of the dress, allowing it to drop in a small arc that, whether by accident or design, brushed the top of the flames.

It was enough.

The hem of the green dress caught instantly, although Brittany did not realize it until a moment later when Kaylee's agonized shriek made her wince. Then she looked back, saw flames climbing toward her hands and dropped the blazing dress, which burst into green and yellow flame in the roaring campfire.

"Awesome!" cried Unknown Boy. Heather laughed with both hands covering her mouth. Everyone else seemed to realize that something unforgivably awful had just happened.

"Oh my God!" whispered Brittany, her face bright with startle.

Kaylee said nothing more, but simply sprinted back down the path and through the Hall backyard. She heard a voice, possibly even several voices, calling her name, but she did not slow down nor did she turn. In a minute she hurtled through the cool darkness on her bike, tears blurring the streetlights as she rode.

Thirteen

Tuesday morning. She felt slow. A check of her watch confirmed it. Five minutes slower than it usually took her to run to Grant Farms. It wasn't until she had closed herself into the lower barn that she began to feel better.

She talked to her horses. They grunted their appreciation or nuzzled her hand or neck. She fed them, brushed them, shoveled their stalls.

This is how the world should be.

She was glad she had agreed to the extra hours. Despite the hard labor, the farm was the happiest, most beautiful place in her life. And the extra hours would help replace the two hundred dollars that she had paid for a dress she would never wear.

A dress that no longer existed.

To make matters worse, Brittany still had Kaylee's $200. She wanted to get it back, but she had been too angry to make another visit to Brittany's house after that awful night. In any case, she would never get what she really wanted. That had been reduced to ash.

She would wear her blue solo dress to the feis this Saturday. It was a good dress—not exactly what she had dreamed of, but a pretty dress. And she would wear her "new" school dress when her ceili team performed.

But that could wait. Now, she had horses to exercise.

On Wednesday, she heard the wheeze in Trooper's breathing.

"It's probably just a little summer virus," said Bob. "I'll call the equine hospital tomorrow and they'll send someone out to take a listen to Trooper's vitals. Good catch, Kaylee."

"Maybe I'll stay a little later tonight," Kaylee suggested. "Make sure Trooper is comfortable, you know."

Bob smiled. "That'd be fine."

Kaylee gave Trooper a good rubdown and covered him with a blanket. She mixed up a special mash for him, but he did not eat much of it, which worried her.

"Look," she told Trooper, "you're pretty stubborn. But don't be stubborn about this silly bug. You're tough. Kick it right out of your system."

Trooper seemed to hang on every word. He bumped her cheek with his warm nose.

"You can't get real sick," she added. "I don't know what I'd do if you did."

When Tom O'Shay arrived later to pick up his daughter, he almost had to carry her to the car.

"I can't go to dance tonight. I'm exhausted."

Mr. O'Shay stroked his daughter's hair as he adjusted her seatbelt. "You don't miss many dance practices." And because of this, he knew she was serious. "I'll call Annie and let her know."

By Friday, however, Trooper had a fever and was congested. Kaylee wondered whether it was something she had done—or had forgotten to do.

"Of course not," Bob said. "It's just like with humans. You can't keep people from getting colds. Sometimes these things hit horses a little harder."

On Saturday morning, Kaylee wanted to call Bob before leaving for the feis to see whether Trooper had improved.

"I know that farmers get up early," said Tom O'Shay, "but you're still not calling him at 6 a.m."

Great, thought Kaylee. *I won't be able to focus on anything else today!*

Their ceili team was the fourth competition on stage three at the feis. Seeing her teammates in their identical school costumes, dazzling makeup and beautiful wigs gave Kaylee some confidence.

We look pretty good!

In their warm-up practicing, Kaylee thought they danced pretty well, too. Even Pearce seemed in sync for a change. "You have all come such a long way," said Miss Helen proudly. "I have no doubt that you will do well."

Once they checked in and were seated beside the stage in the on-deck chairs, Kaylee's confidence fled. Suddenly, images of Trooper lying on the floor of his stall flooded her mind.

It's just nerves. Get over it.

Five ceili teams danced in their competition. Kaylee's group performed second.

Focus! she reminded herself as they finally took their positions on stage. Miss Helen sat stoically in the audience. Then the music started.

"Well," said Miss Helen as they surveyed the results board about an hour after they had finished dancing, "we have some areas to work on, but you can all be proud of bringing home a medal today!"

Kaylee looked at the floor as she said this. She did not feel proud. Everyone on her team had danced well—except for Kaylee.

"I turned the wrong way!" Kaylee complained to Caitlin after they had left the stage. "I did exactly what Pearce did in practice. Only I did it when it mattered!"

"Don't worry about it," said Caitlin philosophically. "Oireachtas is when it matters."

Kaylee shook her head. "We would have won it today if not for me."

"Third place is still pretty good," said Caitlin.

"Out of five?" asked Kaylee.

Caitlin offered an odd little smile. "Lots of people would love to come away from a feis with a third-place medal."

Kaylee grunted. "Not me. We're not going to recall at Oireachtas if I can't remember my steps!"

They had little time to quarrel over this since their reel was set to begin on stage five. Kaylee danced with little enthusiasm, her mind on the ruined dress, on Trooper and on her poor ceili performance.

"I thought you looked fine," said Mrs. Hubbard, who had brought the girls to the feis.

"See?" said Caitlin as they sat alone, waiting for the slip jig to come up. "You're going to do great today."

Kaylee grunted. "Moms are required to say nice things like that, even if you dance awful."

"Not Feis Moms," Caitlin replied.

Feis Mom was a label people applied to mothers who treated every feis like the Olympics. They supervised every step of their child's preparation, looking for a speck of lint or wrinkle in the costume like a frantic drill sergeant, all the while offering nonstop critiques of previous feis performances and instruction on how this feis should be danced. After a dance, they flew back to their child's ear to offer an immediate appraisal, often loud enough for others to hear, frequently focusing on the shortcomings. Then it was off to the results chart, where Feis Mom would jot down the names and numbers of all the place winners so that these foes could be studied and, at some point in the future, crushed.

Kaylee had always been glad that her mother and Mrs. Hubbard were not like that. They were ready with hugs and kind words and seemed to understand that the most important thing about dance was to love it and have fun.

But Kaylee was not having fun today.

"Maybe you need a bagel," said Caitlin. "You're probably suffering from carbohydrate depletion or something."

Kaylee shook her head. Nothing could make her feel better.

"Haven't seen you two for awhile!"

The voice came from behind them, and when Kaylee spun around, she realized that she was wrong. Seeing Riley, the boy from golden Academy, seemed to ignite a tiny spark somewhere in her.

"I've been pretty busy this summer," Kaylee confessed, and she told Riley about her job at Grant Farms and the practicing with her ceili team.

Riley smiled at this news. "You're going to oireachtas? That's great! I've already qualified for solos."

And just like that, as if someone had flipped a switch, the hopeless day had become wonderful. True, they had only gotten third in their ceili, but her mistake was an easy one to correct. Next time would be better. And while Kaylee had not danced particularly well in her reel, she had four other dances. She could still have a successful feis.

And a very cute boy seemed happy that they would be able to spend time together in Columbus at the oireachtas.

"I've got to get over to stage two," Riley announced. "PC starts pretty early at this feis. Maybe you can stop by later and let me know how I look."

Kaylee wanted to let him know how he looked right there.

"He really likes you!" Caitlin giggled as Riley moved out of earshot, and this seemed to bring the day to a completely new and impossible level.

A few minutes later, Kaylee and Caitlin lined up for the slip jig. Usually, this was Kaylee's most difficult step. However, today she felt lighter and more confident than she had for months.

With a bit of a wait in store between the slip jig and the hornpipe, Kaylee suggested that they visit the PC stage. The two arrived to see two fourteen-year-old girls gracefully performing their treble jig in front of the three judges. In the Beginner, Novice and Open Prizewinner levels, only one judge presided over a stage. In PC, scrutinized by a trio, a dancer had little chance that a weakness would not be spotted.

I could be competing against them. They're my age.

Of course, Kaylee needed a first place finish in two more dances before that could happen.

Then they saw Riley, standing in the ready area. In PC, boys and girls competed against each other in most feiseanna, another big difference from the earlier levels. Riley did not wave, but the hint of a smile indicated that he had seen them. In a few minutes, he took the stage alongside a girl wearing a gorgeous yellow dress.

"He's a really good dancer," said Caitlin as Riley finished.

Kaylee was about to agree when she caught sight of the red dress. Brittany Hall took the stage alongside a girl in a pink and white costume, and Kaylee's mood began to shrivel. They congratulated Riley, but then Kaylee stayed behind when Caitlin started back to their camp.

I'm going to get my money.

When Brittany exited the stage and reached the last of the folding chairs set up for spectators, Kaylee was there to meet her. A flicker of surprise was quickly replaced in Brittany's eyes by wary revulsion.

"This is the PC stage, O'Shrimp. You lost?"

Kaylee tried to keep her voice steady, reasonable. "I was wondering when I could get back my $200."

Kaylee thought she detected a flicker of sympathy in Brittany's eyes, but then her face twisted into a sneer. "How about never?"

"But," said Kaylee, rushing to keep up with Brittany as she moved past, "you burned my dress! And I already paid you for it!"

"Wrong!" said Brittany, who did not slow down. "You paid for the dress. I delivered the dress. Then Heather asked to see it. You told me it was okay to give it to her. After that, whatever happened is between you and Heather."

"You're joking, right?" asked Kaylee as Brittany picked up the pace. "I worked hard for that money!"

Brittany stopped suddenly and faced Kaylee. "Do you think Heather understands anything about Irish dance? Do you think she appreciates how much those dresses are worth? How beautiful they are?" Kaylee's mouth opened but nothing came out. Brittany continued. "Do you think it was smart to give your dress to someone who hates your guts and who doesn't care about Irish dance—when she's standing next to a campfire? Maybe next time you should take a little better care of the things you spend your hard-earned money on!"

Then she whirled away and disappeared into the crowd of solo dresses, parents and grandparents.

Kaylee had never felt such anger. She stood unable to move for a minute, not wanting to return to her camp where Caitlin would see her red face and the tears pinched at the corners of her eyes. But underneath the anger was something else, something that made her feel even worse. It was the knowledge that at least part of what Brittany had said was true.

Somehow she finished the rest of her dances. Caitlin could tell that something new was bothering her friend, and Kaylee ultimately confessed what had happened with the dress. Caitlin listened in horror.

"She's just a monster!" said Caitlin. "They both are!"

She pulled Kaylee to a food vendor and bought her a blueberry slush drink. "Maybe this will make you feel better," said Caitlin, who also bought a cherry flavored slush for herself. As they headed toward the results area, the two swung near the PC stage once more and something glittering and familiar on the ground in a camp area caught Kaylee's eye: Brittany's solo dress. It lay spread out on top of a garment bag resting atop a blanket. Several duffel bags and a folding chair defined Brittany's camp amidst a veritable city of similar sites.

Neither Brittany nor her father, who usually accompanied her to feiseanna, was anywhere to be seen.

"I'll meet you at the results," said Kaylee. Caitlin seemed confused, but Kaylee persisted. "I need to check something out."

Now Caitlin smiled as if she understood. "Right! Riley!"

She disappeared through the crowd and Kaylee turned back to Brittany's dress. Caitlin had not noticed it, but to Kaylee, the dress stood out like blood on snow. She knelt beside it. Her revenge would be swift and sweet: pop the top off her blue slush and pour it all over the dress. It would take just a second, and then she would be gone. Many of the families camped in the area seemed to be away at the results area or off at one of the nine stages. The few that remained seemed busy with their own affairs and would think nothing of a girl leaning over a dress bag, which was a perfectly natural thing for a girl at an Irish dance competition to do.

The blueberry stain would never come out. Solo dresses were so delicate that most could not even be dry cleaned.

We'll be even, thought Kaylee. *A dress for a dress.*

She popped the top, gave a final look around. No one was watching. This one moment would make up for so many things: the dress, the broken leg, years of verbal abuse, her aunt's lost medal . . .

And yet, she could not do it.

Inside, she really did not believe the lie that revenge would make it feel all better. She knew that once she stained Brittany's dress, she would simply add guilt to the rest of her miserable baggage.

She stood, found a garbage can, tossed the rest of the slush. Then she headed off toward the results.

Fourteen

World Fest brought hundreds of thousands of people to the Milwaukee lakefront in August of each year. Visitors sampled food vendors who sold everything from baklava to sushi to Chicago-style hot dogs. More than a dozen stages featured such diverse acts as German polka bands, Scottish bagpipe ensembles or English harpists. A "Worldwide Main Street" had been erected where the curious might learn the history of French winemaking or purchase an authentic woolen Irish sweater.

The biggest attraction, however, seemed to be the dance groups. Thousands of people packed themselves onto the benches and bleacher seats around these professional concert venues to watch the Polish men dancers in their striped pants and vests and the women with their crowns of flowers leaping energetically. Or the Russian dancers who brandished swords and thrilled the crowds with their acrobatics. Or the Polynesian dancers who juggled fire while wearing grass skirts.

But the most popular groups of all seemed to be the Irish dancers. And this made Kaylee nervous.

"Miss Helen says there might be more than five thousand people watching us!" she remarked to Caitlin after their final World Fest practice.

Caitlin shrugged. "So? I think there were five thousand in the audience last year when we danced at World Fest."

"Yeah, but last year, we weren't doing our ceili!"

The previous year, Trean Gaoth Academy had staged a marvelous show featuring a stunning variety of dances. Sometimes a dozen dancers in solo costumes had been on stage. At other moments, several ceili teams might be showcasing their meticulous, synchronized movements. Thirty or forty of the youngest dancers would perform a jig, which always drew plenty of smiles and applause. There were even times when almost a hundred dancers would be moving onto or off of the stage simultaneously as the live music kept the crowd clapping. Last year, Kaylee and Caitlin had been part of the almost one hundred dancers, and so they had never really been the sole focus of the crowd's attention. This year, two ceili teams would have the stage all to themselves for a number—and one of them would be Kaylee's team.

"I don't like it," said Kaylee. "It's like Miss Helen keeps looking for new ways to torture us."

"She's just trying to get us ready for oireachtas," said Caitlin reasonably. "If we can handle five thousand people, we ought to be able to handle a couple of old judges."

"I still say it's torture," said Kaylee obstinately. "And she won't be satisfied until she pries the ghillies off my cold, twisted feet!"

This made Caitlin laugh, but the reference to death brought an uncomfortable thought to Kaylee. *I wonder if Miss Helen knows that Lizzie Martin is dead?*

The old woman had never given any indication that this was the case, but it would certainly be an additional reason for her bitterness. Lizzie Martin, her most promising pupil ever, had thrown away her stellar dance career for soccer, and this had taken her to a place where she would die in a car accident. What a waste.

Maybe I should tell her.

The thought just popped into Kaylee's head. But what would that accomplish? Payback? Was she really just looking for a way to torture Miss Helen? And even if her own motives were pure—which Kaylee herself doubted—how would she broach the subject? *Say, Miss Helen, guess what? Remember Lizzie Martin? Just wanted to let you know she's dead. Been that way for fifteen years.*

She shook the idea out of her head and returned to the more critical issue of how she would survive their opening performance at World Fest the next day. Worrying kept her from getting to sleep until after one in the morning.

So much for getting a good night's sleep the night before a performance.

She felt sluggish and achy on her run to the farm on Friday morning. Once she entered the lower barn, however, her mood improved—as it always did. Trooper had mostly recovered from his illness and had resumed his pranks. Methodically, Kaylee cleaned the stalls and fed her friends. When she finished, she felt that she had accomplished something.

This feeling of accomplishment occurred daily at the farm. There was no mystery about it. When she arrived in the morning, the stalls were filthy. A couple hours later, they were clean. She could see that she had made a difference. When the horses were hungry, she fed them. She made a difference to them, too. She brushed them, exercised them, checked them for ticks, removed burrs from their manes.

Not long ago, she had felt this sense of accomplishment about Irish dance. But not at her last feis. She had ruined her ceili team's performance and had earned only a single fourth-place finish in her solo dances. It was hard for her to ever imagine that she might qualify for PC, a dream that had seemed so possible just a couple of months ago. Even in practice she no longer felt the thrill of achievement. Just a couple of months ago, she would regularly practice a new step over and over in her room at home until she mastered it. But there had been no time for extra dance practice lately, not when she spent eight hours of each day at the farm.

She knew that things might be different if she were not working at the farm. Last summer, she had been able to sleep late and devote as many hours as she wanted each day to her Irish dance. On the other hand, she loved Grant Farms. The horses were her friends, and it offered solitude and a kind of peace she had not felt since before her Aunt Kat had died. Of course, the money was nice, too. Kaylee had no desire to return to the days when the answer to every money question had been "no".

When Kaylee arrived home, she just had time to shower and grab her dance bags. Performers needed to arrive an hour before show time at World Fest.

Sitting beside her father, Kaylee hardly said a word all the way to Milwaukee. She was thinking of Trooper, and how it was so much easier shoveling out horse stalls than it was dancing in front of five thousand people.

Why can't Irish dance be easier? Kaylee thought as Tom O'Shay pulled the car into one of the vast, crowded parking lots adjacent to the festival grounds.

Why can't all of life be like the farm?

Fifteen

As Tom O'Shay and his daughter passed through the high, brick-and-iron gateway and onto the festival grounds, the sheer volume of human presence hit Kaylee like an unexpected wave. The closest experience she could relate it to was being in a crowded shopping mall at Christmas. Here, though, everyone wore summer clothing and some carried cardboard boats overflowing with exotic entrees.

Mrs. O'Shay would not be at the Friday show because of her work at the Stitchin' Kitchen, and Will was hardly interested in watching another of his sister's dance performances—not while there were entire worlds to save . . . or pillage. Tom O'Shay consulted a printout and directed Kaylee to the left, where they began weaving themselves into and through the human sea.

"Perfect weather for it," said Mr. O'Shay as they moved through the stream like Irish salmon. "Seventy-five. Not a cloud. You'll definitely have a full house."

This did not cheer Kaylee. She thought about her wrong turn at the last feis. About how she hardly ever practiced at home anymore. About how tired she was.

They arrived at the stage, and Kaylee immediately realized it was one of the largest venues at the festival grounds. An instrumental quartet was singing folk songs to a modest crowd, but Kaylee could see waves of people pouring in, probably anticipating the Irish dance show that would follow.

"Good luck, sweetheart," said her father, kissing the top of her head and handing her the dress bag. "I'm going to grab something to eat, and then I'll be in the audience."

At the back of the giant stage, Kaylee found her Trean Gaoth Academy friends assembling, although most had not donned their dresses yet. Caitlin ran up to her immediately.

"Isn't this exciting?"

Kaylee shivered. "I wish I were home." To herself, she added, *I wish I were at the farm.*

Caitlin gave her a playful shove. "Don't be a party poop! After we dance, we can get fudge!"

"I don't want to mess up again in front of all these people," said Kaylee woefully.

Caitlin's playful expression changed to one of concern. "You're not going to mess up!"

"I did last feis."

Caitlin shook her head. "Everyone goofs up once in awhile. You're going to do great! You're a great dancer!"

Kaylee grunted. "Yeah, right!"

Caitlin looked shocked. "You're one of the best dancers at our school! You're halfway to PC and you work harder than anybody!"

Instead of making her feel better, it had the opposite effect. Is this what Lizzie Martin felt like? Everybody expected so much of her?

"I'll be back," said Kaylee, turning away from the growing number of dancers assembling in the shadow of the outdoor stage.

"Where are you going?" called Caitlin.

"Bathroom," Kaylee shouted back, but that was not true. She needed to get away for just a minute. She needed to think.

Or am I doing too much thinking?

She circled back around to where she had left her father. Tom O'Shay was nowhere in sight, although that was not surprising in this crowd. In any case, Kaylee had no desire to talk to him right now. She walked away from the stage, passed an Italian food vendor, a lemonade wagon and a fruit stand. From the right came Mexican music, and Kaylee headed toward this for no reason whatsoever. As she approached the stage, she saw a large white sign advertising which acts would be performing at various times during the evening. According to the sign, the musicians playing the Mexican music had just started. Kaylee noticed the group that had gone before them:

Golden Academy.

That's the last thing I needed to see right now. Anger and bitterness overwhelmed her.

Her Aunt Kat's medal . . .

The ruined green dress . . .

The $200 that she would never see . . .

So many other cruel injuries.

Yet, the $200 bothered Kaylee most of all. She had worked hard to make the money, but all she had gotten from it was another lesson demonstrating how Brittany Hall always won. It didn't matter whether Kaylee was right and Brittany was wrong. It didn't matter if Kaylee worked harder at dance. It didn't matter if Brittany broke the law or hung out with creeps. It didn't even matter that Brittany had the personality of broken glass. She would always be a better dancer, get the cuter guys, have more money and make life miserable for people like Kaylee.

No, no, no!

Kaylee turned and marched back toward the stage where Trean Gaoth Academy would be performing in half an hour, bumping into people as she strode. Rounding the bleachers that defined the back of the venue, she saw that most of the seats were filled now. Her father had been right. The beautiful August weather had brought everyone out. A high canopy rose above the stage, decked out with the requisite spotlights and the huge speaker system. The folk music had concluded and the crowd nattered restlessly, waiting for the Irish dancers.

When Kaylee reached the back of the stage, she saw that almost everyone from her dance school was now in costume. Caitlin rushed up to her. "Where have you been? You've got to hurry!"

Before Kaylee could say anything, Miss Helen drifted near. "Come on, Kaylee! Get into your school dress so you can run through your dance with the rest of your ceili team!"

Kaylee took a deep breath, and then the words just tumbled out.

"I quit."

Miss Helen's expression suggested that she did not comprehend what Kaylee was saying. "What?"

"I quit. I can't do this anymore. I'm through with Irish dance! It's over!"

And then, without a word of explanation, she turned and walked briskly back the way she had come.

Sixteen

She let Trooper set their course for awhile. Kaylee sat in the saddle and enjoyed the warm sunlight on her face. Then it disappeared as Trooper sought the shade of the tree line along the south edge of the pasture.

"Good boy."

She patted his neck, gave it a quick rub.

"He doesn't really warm up to most folks," Bob had told her of Trooper. "But he sure seems to like you."

This was the best part of working at Grant Farms. When her chores were done, she could exercise the horses by riding them, if she wished. At these moments, she felt loved and happy and in control.

"School will be starting soon," Bob had reminded her recently. "It'd be great if you could come for a few hours after classes every day."

Working hard, getting noticed and getting rewarded for her efforts. That was different.

She had not returned Caitlin's telephone calls for the first few days after World Fest. After Kaylee had stormed away from Miss Helen, she had found her father returning from one of the vendors with some sort of massive sausage covered in sauerkraut.

"Let's go," was all she said, and although he did not understand, he realized that something serious and terrible must have transpired. Some of the details had come out on the trip home. Others when both of her parents had visited her room later that evening.

Naturally she did not tell them everything. No need for them to know about the $200 or her feelings about Lizzie Martin. Mostly she told them that she was tired.

Her parents did not say much. She suspected they were not sure what they *should* say.

During the first phone call she accepted from Caitlin, her friend had expressed shock and concern. "Are you sick? Did you think you were going to throw up?"

By the time they spoke again, Caitlin understood the situation a bit better, and her tone became more urgent, even angry at times. "We got through the dance without you, just like we do in practice when someone's not there. But you can't really be serious about not dancing anymore! What about oireachtas? What are the rest of us going to do?"

Caitlin cried through most of their third phone conversation.

Not going to dance practice felt odd for Kaylee, although it also seemed to liberate her in a sense. She retrieved a box from the basement and filled it with her dance medals and trophies from the top of her dresser. She added her DVD of *Isle of Green Fire* as well as several Irish dance posters, and then she shoved this under her bed. She had begun to ride her bicycle to work again. At the end of her second week without dance, she started to feel normal.

Then came Labor Day weekend and, after that, the start of school.

"This is so cool!" said Jackie during lunch on the first day at Rosemary Senior High. "We're finally freshmen!"

"It's going to be a great year," smiled Kaylee. Thanks to her job at Grant Farms, she had a nice little income. That meant she'd have a social life. And the only pressure she would face would be homework and boys, and there was nothing unusual about that.

Jackie had initially been horrified to learn that Kaylee had quit dance. "It's almost like hearing that Angelo Zizzo retired!" Then, as the first week became more about homework and boys than anything else, this seemed to fade into the background. As Kaylee looked at the family calendar in the O'Shay kitchen the following Friday, she noticed that four weeks had passed since she had walked away from dance at World Fest.

Wow! That went quickly!

She wondered if Miss Helen had found a replacement for her on the ceili team. She would have had to by now. Miss Helen would not simply disband the team.

Would she?

No. She would find another fourteen-year-old dancer, this new dancer would learn the steps, and life would go on. At least she hoped that was what had happened.

During the second week of school, the O'Shays enjoyed a rare family dinner together. The Stitchin' Kitchen had closed at six, Grandma Birdsall was not feeling too tired, Kaylee's father was not off coaching Will's soccer team, and Will was between missions calculated to alternately save and destroy the entire universe. As they passed around second helpings of Mrs.

O'Shay's famous lasagna, Kaylee remembered something that she had been thinking about off and on for a couple of weeks.

"Could I do something to my room?"

Her father looked up from his plate. "What did you have in mind? Paint? Wallpaper?"

Kaylee swallowed a forkful of noodles. "I was thinking it's time for me to get a new rug."

Now Mrs. O'Shay looked up in startle. Will continued shoveling.

"It wouldn't have to be anything fancy. Just something to cover up all that bare wood." When no one said anything right away, she added, "I could help pay for it."

Mrs. O'Shay abruptly left the table and the room without a word.

"I wonder what's up with her?" asked Kaylee. And then a very odd thing happened. Her brother stopped chewing and actually said something during a meal.

"Kaylee, you are such a dork!"

"Let's be nice," cautioned Mr. O'Shay.

"What's that supposed to mean?" Kaylee asked.

"It means you must be an idiot if you can't see how you upset mom!" Will responded.

"Don't call me an idiot!" said Kaylee testily. "I'm not the one who rots his brains all day playing video games!"

"Stop it now, you two," said Tom O'Shay.

"Oh dear," said Grandma Birdsall, dabbing at her mouth with a napkin.

"Well something must be rotting yours," said Will, his voice louder, "because any person of normal intelligence could see that Mom feels bad that you stopped dancing!"

Kaylee immediately dismissed this. "Mom doesn't care if I dance or not."

Will sighed loudly. "You really are dumb!"

"Hey!" shouted Tom O'Shay.

At this, Will turned and headed toward the stairs to his room. After a step, he turned back, grabbed his half full plate, and took it with him.

Kaylee, Grandma Birdsall and her father sat in awkward silence for a few moments. Then Tom O'Shay excused himself to check on his wife.

Kaylee poked at the remaining lasagna noodles on her plate. "Way to go, Will," she muttered to no one in particular. "Way to wreck dinner!"

"I don't think your brother meant any harm," said Grandma Birdsall kindly.

"He was talking like a moron!" Kaylee responded.

"But what he said was true," said Grandma Birdsall calmly. Then she quickly added, "Not the part about you being dumb. Your mother does feel bad that you don't dance anymore."

Kaylee made the I-don't-get-it face. "Why?"

"Because," explained her grandmother, "she wants you to be happy."

"I am happy," said Kaylee.

Grandma Birdsall nodded silently for several moments. "Then your mother will eventually get over it."

Kaylee cleared the supper dishes and moped to her room, noticing that at this particular moment, she did not feel very happy.

Stupid brother. Perhaps she could simply ignore him for the next four years until she went off to college. She'd pretend the little creep didn't exist.

Flopping onto her bed, she realized it was too late to ride her bike out to the farm. Too bad. She could have used some Trooper time.

Kaylee stared at the ceiling for awhile, and then, when she had tried her best to rid her mind of everything troubling, sat up and let her eyes sweep the room. If her mother did not want her to get new carpet, maybe a couple of throw rugs would warm up the place. As her eyes traveled to her dresser, she noticed a medal sitting on top.

I must have missed one when I put the rest in a box.

Perhaps it had fallen on the floor and her mother had set it atop the dresser when she came in to deliver clean laundry. Kaylee slid across the bed. It appeared to be gold. Probably from one of her hard shoe dances. But it seemed smaller than most of her feis medals.

She stood now and looked more closely. Immediately she caught her breath. All Kaylee could utter was a loud, almost painful "Oh!"

She held the medal in her hand. It was real, although she had not been certain at first. A little tarnished, but otherwise it was fine.

Aunt Kat's championship medal.

But how did it get here? It was lost months ago at the soccer fields! We searched and searched.

Kaylee rushed out of her room. "Mom! Dad!"

They were back in the kitchen now. She rushed across the living room and held up her find.

"It's Aunt Kat's medal!" Tears streamed down her cheeks. Her parents moved closer. As they examined the disk, it was clear that they were nearly as stunned as she was.

"You don't know anything about this, do you, Mom?" Mrs. O'Shay asked her own mother.

Grandma Birdsall shook her head and suggested that perhaps it was simply a miracle.

Tom O'Shay threw out another possibility. "Maybe your brother knows something about this."

Kaylee frowned, despite the incredible joy that she felt. "Why would Will know anything? He doesn't even know that the TV has an off button."

Tom O'Shay shrugged. "He lives in this house, too. Either Will knows something, one of us in *this* room is not telling the truth, or we've got a burglar who finds family heirlooms and breaks in to *return* them."

"Or it's a miracle," said Grandma Birdsall, reminding him of the fourth possibility.

Reluctantly, Kaylee ascended the stairs toward Will's lair. Predictably, he was seated on an old, overstuffed chair, eating lasagna and slaughtering aliens.

He frowned as Kaylee stepped quietly into the room. "What do you want?"

She held up the medal. "Do you know anything about this?"

Will's eyes lit up, but then they returned to the screen in front of him. "I don't know anything about anything. My brains are all rotted by video games, remember?"

She took a step closer and knelt down near him. "Don't be stupid!" Then she laughed at the inappropriateness of this response.

Dismal music blared from the TV and Will set down his controller. "I just lost my starship because you distracted me!" Then he looked at the medal again. "Looks like you found it."

"It was on my dresser."

Will looked at it again. "My new science teacher is a complete nerd."

"You two should really get along then."

"Shut up!" Despite himself, Will smiled before continuing. "He was telling us how he finds money and jewelry all the time."

"Is he a detective?"

"No, I told you, he's a nerd! But he's a nice guy nerd. The kind that makes science easier to learn. Anyway, he's got a metal detector and was explaining how it works. And I sort of thought about you."

"You thought about me?" gasped Kaylee. "In eighth grade science class?"

"I remembered how you lost that medal at my soccer game and I knew it meant a lot to you. So I asked Mr. Peters if he ever searched for stuff at the soccer park and he said sometimes. So I told him where you lost the medal and he said he'd look for it the next time he was there."

Kaylee did not know what to say for a moment. Finally she muttered, "Wow," and noticed that her voice cracked a bit. Then she cleared her throat. "By day, a creepy little brother who eats, sleeps and plays video games. By night, a cross between Superman and Angelo Zizzo."

"Angelo Zizzo?"

"That's what Jackie says," Kaylee explained. "She says you look like him."

Will tried unsuccessfully to stifle a smile as he reset his game. "Yeah, well, she's kind of cute for a friend of yours."

Kaylee stood up. "Never, ever say anything like that about any of my friends again. It violates the laws of nature." She turned toward the doorway, took a step, and then turned back and planted a tiny kiss at the top of her brother's head.

Back in her room, Kaylee lay on her stomach on the bed, staring at the medal that represented her Aunt Kat's dreams and, in a way, her *own* dreams.

It had been gone for months. She had given up on it. Now it was back.

And she knew exactly what she had to do.

Seventeen

She laced on her hard shoes, prepared to check in at the stage.

The Milwaukee Snowfeis. The start of a new year. It was always a big event. But this year, it was bigger than ever for Kaylee O'Shay.

She thought about the events of the past four months that had led up to this moment.

It had started with Will finding Aunt Kat's medal. Her Aunt Kat, who had fought so hard for everything, who looked at life as if it were a mountain to be climbed . . .

She had never let adversity keep her from reaching for her dreams. And Kaylee had decided she would not let it hold her back, either.

Kaylee O'Shay loved Irish dance. Yes, it was hard at times. But Kaylee knew that dreams sometimes required sacrifice. And sometimes chasing your dreams hurt. Kaylee had felt a great deal of pain in the past year. Instead of facing it, battling it, she had retreated from it.

Retreated to Grant Farms.

Kaylee loved the farm, too. She loved her horses. Especially Trooper. But she had been using the farm to avoid the pain that sometimes comes with following one's dreams.

The Thursday after Will had given her the medal, Kaylee had returned to Trean Gaoth Academy. Her seven ceili teammates were lacing up their ghillies when she walked in, and they all jumped up to give her hugs.

"You mean," said Kaylee, looking around, "that after five weeks, Miss Helen hasn't replaced me?"

"Of course not," said a rough voice, and Kaylee spun around to see Miss Helen—resplendent in her usual charcoal-colored sweats—standing with her hands clasped behind her.

The seven teammates giggled.

Kaylee felt confused. "But why not?"

"Very simple," said Miss Helen. "I knew you would be back."

Now Kaylee frowned. "After five weeks? There's no way you could have known that."

Miss Helen almost smiled. "That day at World Fest when you told me you were quitting, I knew right away you would come back. You carried your heavy dress bag and your duffel all they way back. If you had truly wanted to quit, you could have dumped it in the nearest trash can."

"I wasn't thinking straight," muttered Kaylee.

"And there is something else," continued Miss Helen, her manner becoming more serious. "It is something inside of you that makes you different. It is a little secret you have."

"I don't have any secrets," protested Kaylee, all the while knowing that she had dozens.

"Everyone has secrets," said Miss Helen. "Your secret is how deeply you love Irish dance. Do you remember that day you spoke harshly to me after class?"

Kaylee blushed, her eyes seeking the wooden floor. How could she forget such a thing?

"It was wrong to do that," continued Miss Helen, "but it showed me how much this means to you. You said, 'I'm not a quitter,' and I knew that you meant it with all of your heart."

Kaylee looked up. "So I can still be on the ceili team for oireachtas?"

"No one will be on a ceili team at oireachtas," said Miss Helen, "if we do not start practicing right now!"

The next two months of training had been some of the best times Kaylee had ever experienced in Irish dance. The eight teammates had gone to movies together, enjoyed a sleepover at Caitlin's house, painted motivational t-shirts for each other, and just plain enjoyed each other's company. Miss Helen had called it learning to be a team. Kaylee had called it friendship.

At the oireachtas, Miss Helen and everyone from Trean Gaoth Academy agreed that they danced an exceptional ceili. "I think that is the best yet," said their teacher. The girls had beamed. Unfortunately, they had not recalled. And while they had been disappointed, this had not crushed them, for they knew they had danced well.

After they posed for pictures in their school dresses at the hotel in Columbus, Kaylee had walked to their room with her mother. "What an awesome week! So many great dancers and beautiful dresses! But you know what was best?"

"What's that, sweetheart?" asked Mrs. O'Shay.

"Pearce has been smiling the whole time!" replied Kaylee. "The only other time I ever saw her smile was our team sleepover!"

Mrs. O'Shay nodded as they approached the elevator. "Well, that little girl has had a pretty rough time of it. She deserves to smile."

Kaylee looked up at her mother, who pushed the call button. "What do you mean?"

"Mrs. Hubbard told me that the poor thing's parents went through a divorce this past year. It really hit Pearce hard. Some weeks she stayed at her dad's house, some weeks at her mom's. What a mess! I guess it was hard for her to sometimes make all the practices, but she danced wonderfully today!"

Now Kaylee understood why Miss Helen had cut Pearce some slack—and why her teacher had been upset when Kaylee hadn't.

As they rode the elevator up, Kaylee explained how she had criticized Pearce. "I'm such an idiot."

"But you two are friends now," her mother pointed out. "We make mistakes. We learn. That's life."

And Kaylee noticed that her mothers eyes were in some far away place.

At least one other noteworthy thing had happened during the fall. Kaylee earned first place finishes in her two remaining dances, which qualified her for PC at the start of the new year.

And so now she stood waiting. Thirty-eight girls would dance in her age group at the Snowfeis. Instead of a single judge, she would face three for the first time. She felt the butterflies.

But she did not let them hurt her. She had made it. She was in PC.

Then she saw the red dress. Brittany Hall paced back and forth, ready to take her place in the line. She spotted Kaylee and, at first, her expression was puzzled. Then amused. Then the eyes darkened and she swished close, speaking in a whisper.

"Prepare to be crushed, O'Shrimp. But don't get used to this. I'm only one first place away from moving up to Champs. And today feels like the day!"

She moved off down the line and Kaylee turned back toward the stage as the music began for the first two girls.

Maybe today was Brittany's day. Perhaps she would win the competition and move up to Champs. As far as Kaylee was concerned, it didn't matter.

"Today is what matters," she said under her breath.

And today, they were both on the same stage.

Acknowledgements

Thanks to My Lovely Wife Marsha, for your help with the manuscript and your unwavering love.

Thanks to my daughter, Haley Marie, whose passion inspired me to write about Irish dance. Thank you for your advice on the manuscript. I am so proud of you—always!

Thank you to my creative writing classes for their feedback.

Thank you to my son, Joshua, for his inspiration.

Thank you to everyone who helped in ways big and small. Even if you were not named here, please know that I am enormously grateful for your contributions.

About the Author

Rod Vick is the author of the Kaylee O'Shay series that began with *Kaylee's Choice*. He has written for newspapers and magazines, has worked as an editor and has taught writing workshops and classes over the span of a quarter century. His short stories have appeared in a variety of literary magazines and have won both regional and national awards. He is currently working on *The Winds of Ireland*, the sixth book in the Kaylee O'Shay series. Mr. Vick was also the 2000 Wisconsin Teacher of the Year.

Rod Vick lives in Mukwonago, Wisconsin with his wife, Marsha, and children Haley and Joshua. An occasional speaker at conferences and orientation events, he also runs marathons, enthusiastically supports his children's dance and soccer passions, and pitches a pretty mean horseshoe.

Kaylee O'Shay, Irish Dancer
Book Six: The Winds of Ireland

For more information about the Kaylee O'Shay series, visit the official online site at www.kayleeoshay.com.

www.ingramcontent.com/pod-product-compliance
Lightning Source LLC
Chambersburg PA
CBHW031445040426
42444CB00007B/987